1 MONTH OF
FREE
READING

at

www.ForgottenBooks.com

By purchasing this book you are eligible for one month membership to ForgottenBooks.com, giving you unlimited access to our entire collection of over 1,000,000 titles via our web site and mobile apps.

To claim your free month visit:
www.forgottenbooks.com/free947801

ISBN 978-0-260-43060-1
PIBN 10947801

This book is a reproduction of an important historical work. Forgotten Books uses
state-of-the-art technology to digitally reconstruct the work, preserving the original format
whilst repairing imperfections present in the aged copy. In rare cases, an imperfection in
the original, such as a blemish or missing page, may be replicated in our edition. We do,
however, repair the vast majority of imperfections successfully; any imperfections that
remain are intentionally left to preserve the state of such historical works.

ANNUAL REPORT

OF THE OFFICERS OF THE

TOWN OF SANDWICH

FOR THE FISCAL YEAR
ENDING JANUARY 31

1939

ANNUAL REPORT

OF THE

OFFICERS

OF THE

TOWN OF SANDWICH

NEW HAMPSHIRE

For the Fiscal Year Ending January 31, 1939

1939

This is to certify that the information contained in this report was taken from official records and is complete to the best of our knowledge and belief.

WILLIAM J. O'BRIEN,
JAMES S. ROGERS,
W. LEROY WHITE,
                                    Selectmen.

January 31, 1939.

List of Town Officers

Moderator
JESSE L. AMBROSE

Representative
PERLEY C. KNOX

Selectmen
CHARLES B. HOYT (Deceased)
JAMES S. ROGERS, 1 year by Appointment
WILLIAM J. O'BRIEN, 2 years, Chairman
W. LEROY WHITE, 3 years

Town Clerk
PERLEY C. KNOX

Tax Collector
LEWIS H. CURRIER

Treasurer
JAMES H. BEEDE

Library Trustees
PERLEY C. KNOX, 1 year
MABEL E. AMBROSE, 2 years
MARY H. COOLIDGE, 3 years

Librarian
BEATRICE BURROWS   ETHEL E. ATWOOD, Asst

Trustees of Trust Funds
JAMES S. ROGERS, 1 yr.   JOHN S. QUIMBY, 2 yrs.
WILLIAM HEARD, 3 yrs.

Cemetery Trustees
WALTER S. TAPPAN, 1 yr.   WILLIAM HEARD, 2 yrs.

Supervisors of Check List
ETHEL F. O'BRIEN   G. ROLAND SMITH
CHARLES J. DAVIS

Ballot Inspectors
Republican
MILDRED M. BLANCHARD
LOUISE C. PEASLEE
E. HAVEN TIBBETTS
PAUL W. TIBBETTS

Democrat
LENORA BICKFORD
WILLIAM HEARD
DORIS L. NIXON

Board of Health
RICHARD H. THOMPSON, M.D., and Selectmen

Forest Fire Wardens
HERBERT L. PERKINS, resigned
G. ROLAND SMITH

Manager Town Hall
G. ROLAND SMITH

Deputies
RYVERS F. AINGER
WALTER H. AVERY
ROSS M. GRAVES
JESSE L. AMBROSE

Constable
JOHN S. QUIMBY

Police
G. ROLAND SMITH

Special Police and Dog Officer
CLARENCE M. BROWN

Notch and Dale Road Agent
G. ROLAND SMITH

Moses Hall Fund Agent
W. ASA BRYANT

Town Road Agents
W. ASA BRYANT
GEORGE W. VITTUM
RALPH Q. PEASLEE

Town Forest Committee
JAMES S. ROGERS
ALONZO McCRILLIS
F. HERBERT WEED

Fire Company
RYVERS F. AINGER, Chief

Auditors
ALISTON H. GRANT   JULIUS H. SMITH, resigned
SUMNER B. CLARK, resigned
CLEVELAND WEED, appointed
HARRY W. CLARK, appointed

SCHOOL DISTRICT OFFICERS
Moderator
JOHN S. QUIMBY

Clerk
WILLIAM HEARD

Treasurer
IDA L. ROGERS

Auditors
JULIUS H. SMITH   SUMNER B. CLARK

School Board
ALICE D. SMITH, 1 yr.   ALISTON H. GRANT, 2 yrs.
GRACE A. AINGER, 3 yrs.

Superintendent
A. W. BUSHNELL

Truant Officer
JOHN S. QUIMBY

School Nurse
EVA M. NELSON, R.N.

Music Teacher
DONALD E. MUSGROVE

Town Warrant

State of New Hampshire   Carroll SS.

To the inhabitants of the Town of Sandwich, in said County and State, qualified to vote in town affairs:

You are hereby notified to meet at the Town Hall in said Town, on Tuesday, the fourteenth day of March, next, at ten o'clock in the forenoon, to act upon the following articles:

1   To see if the town will determine by vote the salary to be paid any of its officers or agents.

2.   To see if the town will authorize the selectmen to borrow money in anticipation of taxes.

3.   To raise and appropriate money to pay the interest on School Fund Note. The sum required is $133.92.

4.   To see if the town will vote to raise and appropriate money for the support of the Library in addition to the amount required by law. The sum recommended to be raised by vote is $420.00.

5.   To see if the town will vote to raise and appropriate money for the observance of Memorial Day. The sum recommended is $100.00.

6.   To see if the town will vote to raise and appropriate money for the observance of Old Home Week. The sum recommended is $150.00.

7.   To see if the town will vote to raise and appropriate the sum of $117.00 to the Lakes Region Association of New Hampshire, for the issuance and distribution of printed matter, calling attention to the resources and natural advantages of the town, in co-operation with other towns in the Lakes Region.

8.   To see if the town will vote to raise and appropriate money for the repair of the Notch and Dale Roads. The sum recommended is $500.00.

9.   To see if the town will accept State Aid for the construction of Class II roads, and raise and appropriate for that purpose the sum of $1759, the State contributing a like amount, or accept Class V assistance and raise and appropriate for that purpose $815.52, the State contributing $3262.09.

10.   To see if the town will vote to raise and appropriate money for the rebuilding of the Jose Bridge at the head of Bennett Street. The estimated cost is $250.00.

11. To see if the town will vote to raise and appropriate money for the repair of highways and bridges and for winter care for the year ensuing, and pass any vote relating thereto. The sum recommended is $8000.00.

12. To see if the town will vote to raise and appropriate money for the construction of a new culvert on the highway near the Charles J. Davis pond. Estimated cost is $300.00.

13. To see if the town will vote to raise and appropriate a sum not exceeding $2000.00 to match such sum or sums as may be available from the State, or others, for the construction of Class II highway and authorize the selectmen to make satisfactory arrangements for the same, if possible.

14. To see if the town will vote to raise and appropriate money for the support of either the Laconia Hospital or Huggins Memorial Hospital at Wolfeboro, or both. The sums recommended are $75.00 for Laconia and $25.00 for Huggins Memorial.

15. To see if the town will vote to raise and appropriate money for the support of the Fire Company. The sum suggested is $400.00.

16. To see if the town will vote to raise and appropriate money for the eradication of the white pine blister. The sum recommended is $100.00.

17. To raise by vote such sum of money as shall be necessary to pay the expense of General Government. The sum recommended is $2400.00.

18. To raise by vote such sum of money as shall be necessary to pay Town Charges for the ensuing year. The sum recommended is $2900.00.

19. To raise and appropirate $1000.00 for the purpose of paying the first annual installment on the $5000.00 loan, without interest, made by Sandwich Town and Grange Fair Association to Town of Sandwich, to help meet emergency highway repairs caused by the Hurricane of September 21, 1938.

20. To see if the town will vote to authorize the selectmen to use money, in their discretion, for the carrying on of relief projects, to be used either with state or federal funds, and to raise and appropriate money for the same. The sum suggested is $1000.00.

21. To hear the report of the Zoning Commission and take any action relating thereto.

22. To see if the town will vote to raise and appropriate the sum of $30.00 for the purpose of paying its proportionate share budget deficit for Recreational Extension Service.

23. To choose all necessary town officers for the year ensuing.

Given under our hands and the seal of the Town of Sandwich, this twenty-seventh day of February, A.D. 1939.

A true copy, Attest

WILLIAM J. O'BRIEN,
JAMES S. ROGERS,
W. LEROY WHITE,

[SEAL]   Selectmen of Sandwich.

Budget for 1939

State Tax		$2,940.00
County Tax, estimated		8,000.00
School District Budget		12,766.99
General Town Government:		2,400.00
Town Officers' Salaries	$963.00	
Town Officers' Expenses	800.00	
Election and Registration	75.00	
Town Hall	562.00	
Town Charges:		3,050.00
Police	$300.00	
Forest Fires	100.00	
Health and Vital Statistics	50.00	
Public Welfare:	2,350.00	
Old Age Assistance	$700.00	
Town Poor	1,500.00	
Soldiers' Aid	150.00	
Interest	250.00	
Highways and Bridges:		8,000.00
Snow	$4,000.00	
Summer Care	3,000.00	
General	500.00	
Bushes	500.00	
Notch and Dale Road (Leg. Special)		500.00
Town Road Aid (T.R.A.)		815.52
New Construction (Class II Roads)		2,000.00
Library by Law, estimated		73.50
Library by Vote		420.00
Support of Fire Company		400.00
Observance of Memorial Day		100.00
Observance of Old Home Week		150.00
Blister Rust		100.00
Interest on School Fund Note		133.92
Support of Hospitals		100.00
Lakes Region Association		117.00
Relief Projects		1,000.00
One Year Payment, acct. Sandwich Fair Asso. Note		1,000.00
Article X—Jose Bridge		250.00
Article XII—Box Culvert		300.00
Total		$44,616.93

Summary Inventory

APRIL 1, 1938

Land and buildings	$1,109,916.00
Electric lines	15,162.00
95 horses	5,836.00
34 oxen	2,764.00
231 cows	10,104.00
28 neat stock	866.00
76 sheep	340.00
1225 fowl	980.00
3 boats and launches	210.00
Wood and lumber	8,670.00
Gasoline, pumps and tanks	1,216.00
Stock in trade	15,360.00
Mills and machinery	2,364.00
Total valuation exclusive of exemptions	$1,173,778.00
Soldiers' exemptions	10,970.00
Total valuation	$1,184,748.00

Appropriations and Taxes for 1938

General government	$2,300.00
Fire Department	500.00
Blister Rust	100.00
Laconia Hospital	150.00
Huggins Memorial Hospital	50.00
Town Road Aid	817.87
Town Maintenance	7,500.00
Notch and Dale, Leg. Special	500.00
Squam Lake, Special	2,000.00
Library	493.50
Town charges	1,200.00
Memorial Day and Old Home Week	225.00
Interest on School Fund Note	133.92
State Tax	2,940.00
County Tax	7,922.61
School Tax	12,581.00
To meet State and Federal Projects	1,000.00
Lakes Region Association	128.00

Total Appropriations		$40,541.90
Less Estimated Revenue		
Interest and Dividend Tax	$4,833.98	
Insurance Tax	16.50	
Railroad Tax	25.65	
Savings Bank Tax	1,300.00	
Motor Vehicle Permits	$1,000.00	7,176.13
		33,365.77
Plus Overlay		709.52
Less National Bank Stock Tax $26.75		34,075.29
474 Poll Taxes	948.00	974.75
Amount to be Raised by Property Taxes		$33,100.54

TAXES COMMITTED TO COLLECTOR

Property taxes	$33,100.54	
474 Poll taxes	948.00	
National Bank Stock Tax	26.75	
		$34,075.29
Additional taxes for 1938 and 1937		52.56
Total Tax Committed to Collector		$34,127.85
Town Tax Rate, per $100.00	$2.82	

Financial Report

ASSETS

Cash
In hands of Treasurer $2,635.92
In hands of officials
    Mabel E. Ambrose, Lib. Trustee   235.26
    Beatrice Burrows, Librarian   5.06
    James H. Beede, Treas.
      Old Home Assn.   .63
    Ryvers F. Ainger, Fire Chief   358.15
    Selectmen, Blister Rust balance   .42
Trustees of Trust Funds
    Moses Hall Fund $766.96
    Sandwich Fair Fund   112.27
    D. D. Atwood, Sidewalk Fund   18.20

                               897.43

Accounts Due Town
From State
    Joint Highway Construction Acct. 6.97
From County
    For County Poor   155.77
Other Bills Due Town
    Chas. B. Hoyt Est.
      Bal. Veterans' Assn.   38.69
Unredeemed Taxes (Tax sales)
Levy of 1938   317.54
          1937   73.61
          1936   81.06
Previous years   103.64

Total Assets   4,910.15
Excess Liabilities over Assets   2,656.46

Grand Total $7,566.61
Surplus, January 31, 1938   5,077.07
Net Debt, January 31, 1939   2,656.46
    Debt created for purpose of meeting Liabilities for
    Hurricane Road Damage.

LIABILITIES

Accounts Owed by Town
 Outstanding bills $40.87
 Due School District
  1938 Dog Licenses   220.09
State and Town Joint Highway Accounts
 a. Unexpended balance in State
  Treasury   6.97
 b. Unexpended balance in Town
  Treasury   4.64
Long Term Notes Outstanding
 Sandwich Town and Grange Fair
  Association, without interest, to
  meet Emergency Hurricane
  Liabilities   5,000.00
Trust Fund Accounts
 Moses Hall Fund,
  Balance in Treasury   62.04
 School Fund Note   2,232.00

  Total Liabilities $7,566.61
  Grand Total $7,566.61

Schedule of Town Property

Town Hall, lands and buildings	$7,100.00
Furniture and equipment	1,250.00
Library, land and building	17,500.00
Furniture and equipment	8,000.00
Fire Department	
Apparatus and equipment	5,500.00
Highway Department	
Lands and buildings	200.00
Equipment	700.00
Parks, commons and playgrounds	1,500.00
Schools	
Land and Buildings	17,500.00
Equipment	2,300.00
	$61,550.00

1938 Town Clerk's Report

1937 Dog Licenses received after
Jan. 31, 1938:

7 male dogs	$14.00	
1 female dog	5.00	
	$19.00	
Town Clerk's Commission	1.60	
		· $17.40

1938 Dog Licenses:

One 5 dog Kennel	$12.00	
One 10 dog Kennel	25.00	
85 male dogs	170.00	
4 female dogs	20.00	
	$227.00	
Town Clerk's Commission	18.20	
		208.80

Taxes on Motor Vehicles:

361 permits for 1938	$1,127.79	
13 permits for 1939	134.34	
		1,262.13
		$1,488.33

Town Treasurer's Report

IN ACCOUNT WITH THE TOWN OF SANDWICH, N. H.

DR.

Received from Treasurer, 1938	$6,826.13
Received from Lewis H. Currier, Collector	34,127.85
Received from Treasurer of N. H.	6,877.94
Received from Quimby Trustees	1,000.00
Received from William Heard, Trustee of Trust Funds	2,017.31
Received from Meredith Village Savings Bank, loan	3,000.00
Received from Sandwich Fair Association, loan	5,000.00
Received from Selectmen, redeemed taxes	41.81
Received from Selectmen, miscellaneous	2,025.82
	$60,916.86

CR.

Paid State Tax	$2,940.00
Paid County Tax	7,922.00
Paid Schools	12,936.00
Paid Highways	23,059.17
Paid Library	493.50
Paid Town Poor	1,543.30
Paid Old Age Assistance	684.01
Paid Bounties	37.80
Paid Old Home Association	150.00
Paid Memorial Day	109.10
Paid Abatements	278.11
Paid Sandwich Fire Dept.	500.00
Paid Meredith Savings Bank, Loan and interest	3,063.25
Paid Miscellaneous	4,564.70
Cash on hand, Jan. 31, 1939	2,635.92
	$60,916.86

JAMES H. BEEDE,
Treasurer.

Collector of Taxes

SANDWICH, N. H.

February 11, 1939.

To the Selectmen of the Town of Sandwich:
As Tax Collector of the Town of Sandwich, I hereby submit the following report for the year 1938.

Amount of Warrant	$34,075.29	
Amount of Added Taxes for 1938	34.56	
Amount of Added Taxes for 1937	14.00	
		$34,123.85
Amount of Taxes collected	33,845.74	
Amount of Abatements	278.11	
		$34,123.85

ABATEMENTS

Fred Boyd, address unknown	$2.00
Fred N. Burrows, error in assessment	5.64
George O. Cook, over 70 years	2.00
Charles S. Cram, adjustment	.57
Elizabeth Crockett, over 70 years	2.00
Everett Davey, under 21 years	2.00
Minnie L. Demick, deceased	2.00
Harvey O. Dennis, discharged veteran	2.00
Pauline E. Dennis	2.00
Harold Denny	2.00
Alice Denny	2.00
Est. of Nellie F. Eastman, Error in assessment	33.84
George L. Eaton, over 70 years	2.00
Harry O. Haley, by order of selectmen	69.65
Adelaide J. Marston, over 70 years	2.00
Dorothy M. Martin paid in Manchester, N. H.	2.00
Clifford Mathews, left town	2.00
Marjorie Mathews, left town	2.00
Jesse A. Mudgett	2.56
Jennie E. Mudgett	2.00
Grace LeCroix Ogden	2.00
Helen Pettingill paid in Meredith, N. H.	2.00
Grace Plume, left town	2.00
George Scriggins, over 70 years	2.00

Eva G. Smith	2.00
Elizabeth Weed, resident in Massachusetts	2.00
Edson W. Worthen	2.00
Weldon W. Worthen	4.82
Heirs of George A. Collins, adjustment	1.41
Rev. Edward R. Welles, error in assessment	31.02
Hale House Ass'n, error in warrant	84.60
Total Abatements	$278.11

RECORD OF TAX SALE

Name of owner	Amount of Tax	Costs	Name of Buyer
J. Frank Atwood	$59.22	$3.06	Town
Jennie M. Avery	75.32	3.06	Town
Mildred McCrea	4.82	3.06	Town
Wallace Nudd	26.56	3.06	Town
Clarence Robinson	12.18	3.06	James Beede
Marjorie V. Sargent	50.76	3.06	Town
Henry H. Bennett	2.82	3.06	Town
Mathew M. Blunt		3.06	Town
Mary A. Flood	28.20	3.06	Town
Forest Products Co.	42.30	3.06	Town
Heirs of Carlos Huckins	bal. 7.05	3.06	Wm. A. Brown & Chas. N. Swayne

RECORD OF 1937 TAXES SOLD TO TOWN AND REDEEMED IN 1938

Name of owner	Amount of Tax	Costs	Redeemed By
Walter Bryant	$39.75	$2.06	Frank A. Bryer

RECORD OF 1937 TAXES SOLD AND UNREDEEMED

Name of owner	Amount of Tax	Costs	Name of Buyer
Forest Products Co.	$39.75	$2.06	Charles B. Hoyt
Watson B. Flett	2.65	2.06	Charles B. Hoyt

I hereby certify that the above report is correct to the best of my knowledge and belief.

LEWIS H. CURRIER,
Tax Collector.

Summary Receipts

Current Revenue
  From Local Taxes
    Property Taxes actually

collected	$32,892.99	
Poll taxes collected	930.00	
National Bank Stock taxes	26.75	
Total of year's collections		$33,849.74
Abatements paid by Town		278.11
Tax sales redeemed		41.81
From State		
Reimbursement for Welfare		
payments	108.14	
Interest and dividends tax	4,502.90	
Insurance tax	16.50	
Railroad tax	23.21	
Savings Bank tax	1,231.81	
Use of grader	10.00	
Abatement State tax (Nat. Forest)	723.88	
Bounties	77.20	
		6,693.64
From County		
For support of poor		100.60
From Local Sources Except Taxes		
Dog licenses	226.20	
Business licenses and permits	19.00	
Rent of town property	206.50	
Income from trust funds	2,112.94	
Registration of Motor		
Vehicles, 1938	1,127.79	
Registration of Motor		
Vehicles, 1939	134.34	
National forest reserve	184.30	
		4,011.07
Receipts Other Than Current Revenue		
Temporary loan	3,000.00	
Long term note	5,000.00	
Refunds	115.76	
Gifts	1,000.00	
		9,115.76
Total Receipts from all Sources		$54,090.73
Cash on hand February 1, 1938		6,826.13
Grand Total		$60,916.86

Summary Payments

General Government
  Town officers 'salaries $963.00
  Town officers' expenses 771.79
  Election and registration expenses 116.84
  Town Hall and other buildings 846.70
Protection of Persons and Property
  Police Department 435.92
  Fire Department 772.55
  Blister Rust 101.25
  Bounties 37.20
  Damage by dogs 6.11
Health
  Health department, hospitals 282.10
  Vital statistics 10.90
Highways and Bridges
  Town Maintenance,
    including bushes 4,384.30
  Snow Removal, including sanding 5,332.24
  Town Road Aid 820.48
  Hurricane Account 7,513.32
  General Expenses of Department 561.22
  Notch and Dale Roads
    (Leg. Special) 495.36
Libraries 493.50
Charities
  Old Age Assistance 683.73
  Town Poor 1,332.81
  County Poor 228.07
Patriotic Purposes
  Memorial Day and
  other celebrations 265.10
  Aid to soldiers and their families 144.75
Public Service Enterprises
  Wood Cutting Project #1460 82.49
  Road Widening Project #1404 1,008.93
Unclassified
  Lakes Region Association 128.00
  Taxes bought by town 317.54
  Discounts and Abatements 278.11
Interest on temporary loan 63.25
New Construction and Improvements
  Squam Lake Road 1,999.89
  Water holes 36.60
  Moses Hall Fund 960.23
Indebtedness
  Temporary loan 3,000.00
  Refund 8.66

Payments to Other Governmental Divisions
    Taxes paid to State   2,940.00
    Taxes paid to County   7,922.00
    Payment to School Districts 12,936.00

Total Payments for all Purposes $58,280.94
Cash on hand January 31, 1939   2,635.92

    Grand Total $60,916.86

Detail Statement of Receipts

CURRENT REVENUE

From Local Taxes
Property taxes for 1938
  actually collected $32,892.99
456 Poll taxes for 1938 912.00
National Bank Stock taxes 26.75

$33,831.74

7 Additional Poll Taxes for 1937,
  paid Collector 14.00
2 Poll Taxes for 1937,
  paid Selectmen 4.00

18.00

Selectmen's Abatement Order 278.11
Tax Sales Redeemed,
Frank A. Bryer, Walter C. Bryant Place 41.81

From State
Reimbursement for Direct Relief 108.14
Interest and Dividends Tax 4,502.90
Insurance Tax 16.50
Railroad Tax 23.21
Savings Bank Tax 1,231.81
Use of Grader 10.00
Abatement State Tax for
  Nat. Forest 723.88
Bounties 77.20

6,693.64

From County
Assistance to Wilfred Sturgeon 5.24
Assistance to Roland Summers 7.06
Assistance to James Sullivan 55.00
Refund for Relief in 1937 28.30
Assistance to Victor L. Whiting* 5.00

100.60

From Local Sources, Except Taxes
Dog Licenses
  7 Males for 1937 12.60
  1 Female for 1937 4.80
  85 Males for 1938 153.00
  4 Females for 1938 19.20
  1 5-dog kennel 11.80
  1 10-dog kennel 24.80

226.20

* Repaid by Applicant.

Business Licenses and Permits
Watson E. Beach, 1 pool table | 10.00
Chas. J. Davis, filing fee | 1.00
G. Roland Smith, filing fee | 1.00
Perley C. Knox, filing fee | 2.00
Ethel F. O'Brien, filing fee | 1.00
Wm. J. O'Brien, filing fee | 2.00
Guy B. Torsey, filing fee | 2.00

19.00

Rent of Town Property
Town Hall
4 Pictures | 20.00
3 Local Plays | 15.00
11 Basketball games | 31.50
42 Dances | 126.00
1 Lodge | 3.00
Evan Show | 6.00
Miscellaneous | 5.00

206.50

Income from Trust Funds
Blanchard Highway Fund | 1,212.97
Moses Hall Fund | 899.97

2,112.94

Automobile Permit Fees
361 Permits for 1938 | 1,127.79
13 Permits for 1939 | 134.34

1,262.13
National Forest Reserve | 184.30

Receipts Other Than Current Revenue
Temporary Loan in
anticipation of Taxes, Meredith
Village Savings Bank | 3,000.00
Long Term Notes
Sandwich Town and Grange
Fair Ass'n, payable $1,000.00
annually | 5,000.00

Refunds

Ryvers F. Ainger duplicate payment | 14.40
Cash from Est. of N. F. Gilman | 4.41
Perley C. Knox, Adjustment for
1937 acct. | .20
Victor Whiting Repayment for
assistance | 5.00

Daniel Clark, W.P.A. pay advance   39.55
Orrin Tilton, Labor adjustment   11.20
Cleveland Weede, purchase of
   Cement   21.00
Frederic G. Pearson, W.P.A.
   Sponsors contribution   20.00
Gifts
   Quimby Trustees for
     Quimby Bridge   1,000.00

Total Receipts, other than Current Revenue   9,115.76

Total Receipts from all sources   54,090.73
Cash on hand Feb. 1, 1938   6,826.13

     Grand Total $60,916.86

Detail Statement of Payments

CURRENT MAINTENANCE EXPENSES

General Government

Town Officers' Salaries—

William J. O'Brien, Chm. Selectmen	200.00
James S. Rogers, Selectman	150.00
W. Leroy White, Selectman	150.00
Lewis H. Currier, Tax Collector	150.00
James H. Beede, Treasurer	100.00
Perley C. Knox, Town Clerk	50.00
Ralph Q. Peaslee, Road Agent	25.00
W. Asa Bryant, Road Agent	25.00
George W. Vittum, Road Agent	25.00
Clarence M. Brown, Dog Officer	25.00
Ethel F. O'Brien, Supervisor	13.00
G. Roland Smith, Supervisor	13.00
Robert Woodward, Supervisor	10.00
Aliston H. Grant, Auditor	9.00
Cleveland Weed, Auditor	9.00
Harry W. Clark, Auditor	9.00

$963.00

Town Officers' Expenses—

Lewis H. Currier, Travel and Supplies	125.00
Perley C. Knox, 374 Auto Permit Fees	93.50
Perley C. Knox, Office Supplies	9.40
Perley C. Knox, Attendance at Meetings	10.00
Reuben N. Hodge, Town Officers' Bonds	100.00
Blanchard Printing Co., Reports	248.05
Edson C. Eastman Co., Office Supplies	33.00
W. H. Forristall, Receipts	5.00
Robert S. Quinby, M.D. 2 medical exams.	15.00
Evans Printing Co., Stationery	1.58
Carroll W. Stafford, Probate records	.10
Chas. H. Carter, List of Conveyances	14.86
J. H. Forster, Repair adding machine	3.50
N. H. Assessors Assn., annual dues	2.00
S. W. Heard, stamps	3.00
Meredith Trust Co., Box Rent	5.50

William Heard, Trustee, Postage	2.50
James H. Beede, Office Supplies	6.73
James S. Rogers, 4 trips	20.00
James S. Rogers,	
Keys for Town Hall	.70
James S. Rogers, Telephone	.80
William J. O'Brien, 4 trips	21.10
William J. O'Brien,	
Telephone and Stamps	3.67
W. Leroy White, 5 trips .	27.00
Copying tax invoice	12.00
Postage	7.80

$771.79

Election and Registration Expenses—

Blanchard Printing Co., Ballots	25.00
Mabel E. Ambrose, dinners	1.50
Glenn Smith, lunches	1.31
Perley C. Knox, lunches	2.00
Isabel Smith, lunches	8.40
Edson C. Eastman Co.,	
Tally sheets	10.13
Haven Tibbetts, Ballot Clerk	15.00
Louise C. Peaslee, Ballot Clerk	5.00
Paul W. Tibbetts, Ballot Clerk	13.50
Mildred M. Blanchard, Ballot Clerk	10.00
William Heard	20.00
Lewis H. Currier	5.00

116.84

Expenses of Town Hall—

G. Roland Smith, Janitor Service	125.00
G. Roland Smith, Work on Wood	12.90
G. Roland Smith, Pipe and damper	3.15
White Mountain Power Co.,	
Electricity	100.00
N. E. Telephone & Telegraph Co.	
Telephone	75.00
J. B. Varick & Co., Supplies	32.99
Ford Foundry Co., Stove	29.70
Melcher & Prescott, Insurance	218.75
Cecil Talbot, cleaning hall	38.40
West Disinfecting Co., Floor finish	29.16
Diamond Match Co., 2 gal. Benzol	1.96
E. I. Hamilton, Supplies	5.81
Chas. C. Rogers Co.,	
Office Equipment	36.90
James S. Rogers, Scenery	55.00

Arnall's Trading Post, Supplies   1.50
Guy B. Torsey, Labor on floor   10.00
John St. Clair, Tuning Piano   4.00
Grant Hodsdon, floor wax   5.40
Glenn Smith, supplies   2.05
Fred A. Bickford, 8 cds. wood   52.50
Irvine's Express, cartage   6.53

$846.70

Protection of Persons and Property

Police Department, Including Tramps—

Clifton J. Goodwin, care 157 tramps	235.50
Grace S. Ford, 43 tramps	65.50
Daniel Clark, Tilton case	42.00
Wm. J. O'Brien, Tilton case	8.00
James S. Rogers, Tilton case	5.00
G. Roland Smith, Police	24.90
J. B. Varick Co., paint for life boat	7.92
W. D. Huse & Sons, boat fittings	12.84
D. Irvine, anchor and cartage	3.25
Glenn Smith, Boat supplies	.80
G. B. Torsey, building and setting life preserver shelters	15.88
South Tamworth Industries, materials for same	12.03
F. R. Prescott, materials	.38
Arnall's Trading Post, shellac	1.03
J. P. Pitman, Rope, etc.	.89

$435.92

SELECTMEN'S OFFICE
CENTER SANDWICH, NEW HAMPSHIRE

Thomas McGowan, for over 20 years a summer resident of Sandwich, presented his boat, life preservers and grappling irons to the Town for use at the Squam Lake bathing beach, in memory of his son, Tom.

His gift also made it possible to provide the beach at Bearcamp Pond with life preservers.

The Town has erected suitable housing stands for the equipment and a mooring for the boat.

It is hoped that our young folks will understand the purpose for which the boat is moored at the beach, and will not use it except for emergency purposes.

A McKesson Resuscitator has been added to the above equipment, the fund for same being augmented by the efforts of Curtis Arnall and a group of associate Radio Entertainers with local talent who presented plays for that purpose.

In behalf of the Town we wish to extend thanks.

Fire Department—
Sandwich Fire Co., Appropriations	500.00	
Tamworth Fire Co., Briggs fire	89.00	
Herbert L. Perkins, Payroll,		
Watson fire	51.00	
Payroll, Peaslee fire	29.00	
176 Fire permits	44.00	
Jesse L. Ambrose,		
Rent of Baptist sheds	10.00	
State of N. H.		
Forest fire equipment	30.00	
F. W. Burrows,		
Express and cartage of same	1.90	
G. Roland Smith, 16 fire permits	4.00	
Posting notices	5.20	
Robert Woodward, Fire hazard work	8.45	
		$772.55

Blister Rust—
John H. Foster, State forests	100.00	
Lawrence Blumberg, Sub. foreman	1.25	
		101.25

Bounties—
William J. O'Brien, 58 hedgehogs	11.60	
James S. Rogers, 29 hedgehogs	5.80	
W. Leroy White, 27 hedgehogs	5.40	
2 bears	10.00	
W. L. White, Exec. Will of C. B. Hoyt,		
22 hedgehogs	4.40	
		37.20

Dog Damage—
Edson C. Eastman Co., 125 tags		6.11

Health Department—
Richard H. Thompson, M. D.,		
Measles quarantine	82.10	
Laconia Hospital, Appropriation	150.00	
Huggins Memorial Hospital,		
Appropriation	50.00	
		282.10

Vital Statistics—
Preston B. Smart, 9 Probate returns	.90	
Perley C. Knox, recording 16 births,		
21 deaths, 7 marriages	10.00	
		10.90

Highways and Bridges

EAST DISTRICT, GEORGE W. VITTUM, AGENT

(HIGHWAY ACCOUNT)

MAINTENANCE

George W. Vittum, truck	$446.40
George W. Vittum	278.50
George W. Vittum, Jr.	87.20
William Vittum	45.60
Herbert Nelson	45.40
Clifton Goodwin	36.80
E. Martel	35.20
Charles Tilton	12.80
Edwin Jeffers	11.20
Wilbur Martin	11.20
Harry Haley	6.40
Orrin Tilton	6.40
Albert Brownlie	4.80
Francis Mudgett	3.60
Kenneth Nelson	2.80
Marshall W. Vittum, gravel	8.00
Sandwich Gen. Store, spikes	2.00
Henry Estes, gravel	.75
Arthur Abbott, gravel	.60
Fred O. Mason, gravel	.45
George Pease, gravel	.30
Herbert Perkins, gravel	.30

Total $1,046.70

BUSHES

George Vittum, truck	38.40
Wilfred Stone	31.00
William Stone	31.00
George W. Vittum	30.50
William Davison	22.40
Theodore Wallace	22.40
Fred Barnes	20.80
Harold Nelson	19.20
Forest Martel	16.00
E. Martel	16.00
Archie Palmer	14.80
James Prescott	13.20
Ralph Manning	12.80
Edson Taylor	12.80
Harry Haley	8.00
Albert Brownlie	6.40
Thomas Nelson	5.20

Wm. Vittum	3.60	
Albert Gale	3.20	
William O'Brien, Jr.	2.40	
James Nixon	1.60	
Total		$331.70

SNOW REMOVAL

William Nelson, truck and plow	$360.50	
George W. Vittum	64.50	
George W. Vittum, Jr.	25.60	
George W. Vittum, truck	23.20	
Harold Nelson	17.60	
Thomas Nelson	17.60	
Herbert Nelson	7.20	
Wilbur Martin	5.60	
Kenneth Vittum	3.60	
Forest Martel	2.00	
Walter Granville	1.20	
Harold Pickering	1.20	
Total		$529.80

SANDING

George W. Vittum, truck	$103.20	
George W. Vittum	58.00	
George W. Vittum, Jr.	27.20	
Herbert Nelson	23.20	
Orrin Tilton	9.60	
Thomas Nelson	6.40	
Meredith Grain Co., salt	19.40	
Marshall Vittum, gravel	9.36	
Total		$256.36
Total East District—Highway Account		$2,164.56

NORTH DISTRICT, RALPH Q. PEASLEE, AGENT
HIGHWAY ACCOUNT
MAINTENANCE

Ralph Peaslee, truck	$386.40
Ralph Peaslee	251.75
Albert Brownlie	88.00
Harry Wallace	82.00
Roland Peaslee	81.60
Wilbur Cook	74.60
John Campbell	32.80
George McCormack	26.60
Irving Mudgett	17.80
Roscoe Peaslee	15.60
Everett Davey	12.80
Wilfred Plummer	8.00

Fred Barnes	6.40
August Blodgett	6.40
William Stone	5.80
Everett Campbell	5.60
Wesley Tewksbury	3.60
Frank Burrows	3.20
John Callahan	3.20
Robert Peaslee	3.20
Clarence Brown	2.40
Lester Moody, gravel	5.00
Will Plummer, gravel	3.60
John Bryant, supplies	3.10
Harry Wallace, gravel	1.90
Harry Clark, gravel	1.50
South Tamworth Industries	
bolts and lumber	1.14
William Hurd, gravel	1.00
Ralph Peaslee, culvert clamp	.81
William Nelson, bolts	.50

Total		$1,136.30

BUSHES

Ralph Peaslee	$52.75	
Ralph Peaslee, truck	41.20	
Roger Plummer	45.40	
Everett Campbell	44.60	
George McCormack	43.60	
Harry Wallace	42.20	
John Campbell	38.20	
Robert Peaslee	19.20	
Elmer Elliott, team	2.63	
Total		$329.78

SNOW REMOVAL

Elmer Thompson, tractor	$270.75	
Ralph Q. Peaslee, truck	16.00	
Ralph Q. Peaslee	14.00	
Albert Brownlie	15.20	
Roscoe Peaslee	15.20	
Wilbur Cook	4.80	
Wilfred Plummer	3.20	
Roland Peaslee	1.60	
William Stone	.40	
Total		$341.15

SANDING

Ralph Q. Peaslee, truck	$167.20
Ralph Q. Peaslee	85.75
Wilfred Plummer	42.00

Irving Mudgett	31.60
Arthur Watson	26.20
Frank Burrows, truck	19.20
George McCormack	17.60
Roscoe Peaslee	16.80
Albert Brownlie	15.20
Everett Campbell	14.80
Wilbur Cook and truck	9.60
Clarence Brown	6.00
Howard Stevenson	3.20
Gerald Atwood	2.80
John Campbell	2.60
Clifton Campbell	1.60
Cora Remick, gravel	21.20
John Bryant, supplies	9.70

Total $493.05

Total North District—Highway Account $2,300.28

WEST DISTRICT, W. ASA BRYANT, AGENT, HIGHWAY ACCOUNT
MAINTENANCE

W. Asa Bryant, truck	$381.60
W. Asa Bryant	289.00
Frank Mudgett	125.60
Guy Avery	72.20
Robert Mudgett	41.20
Otis Cook	39.00
Robert Penniman	24.80
Richard Gray and truck	22.80
Clarence Robinson, truck and horses	21.90
Dewey Hamilton	16.20
Frank Burrows	13.40
Norman Hodge	12.80
Newell Burrows	12.40
Elisha Mudgett	10.80
Elwood Mudgett	10.00
Roger Plummer	10.00
Chester Burrows	9.60
Frank Martin	8.20
Sumner Taylor	6.80
Charles Mudgett	6.40
Eugene Fogg	5.80
Leon Smith	5.20
John Martin	5.00
James Beede	4.60
Arthur Lewis and truck	3.60
Ernest McDonald	3.80

Arthur Avery and horses	3.50	
Roland Jackson	3.48	
George Eaton	3.20	
Roger Deming	3.20	
Wilbur Mudgett	3.20	
Clarence Plummer	3.20	
Arthur Tuttle	3.20	
Nathaniel Burrows	1.60	
Richard Gray	1.60	
Edson Worthen	1.00	
So. Tamworth Industries, plank.	18.90	
John Bryant, spikes and explosives	2.56	
E. I. Hamilton, spikes	1.18	
William Nelson, labor	.80	
Nelson's Garage, road machine	.50	
Total		$1,213.82

BUSHES

W. Asa Bryant	$36.00	
W. Asa Bryant, truck	30.40	
Charles Mudgett	30.40	
Frank Mudgett	30.40	
Eugene Fogg	20.80	
Guy Avery	19.20	
Roger Deming	17.80	
Fred Barnes	17.60	
Richard Gray	17.60	
Clarence Robinson	16.00	
Elwood Mudgett	14.40	
Chester Burrows	12.80	
Alexander Hamilton	12.80	
Wilbur Mudgett	11.40	
Edson Worthen	11.20	
Theodore Wallace	11.20	
Elmer Moody	9.60	
William Davison	6.40	
Total		$326.00

SNOW REMOVAL

W. Asa Bryant and truck	$19.20	
W. Asa Bryant	12.00	
Frank Mudgett	9.60	
Richard Gray	7.60	
Jeremiah Martin	6.40	
Elisha Mudgett	2.00	
Total		$56.80

SANDING

W. Asa Bryant, truck	$89.66
W. Asa Bryant	38.50
Fred Mudgett, truck	80.40
Fred Mudgett	42.25
Frank Mudgett	44.60
Norman Moulton	27.00
Otis Cook	22.60
Arthur Lewis and truck	19.80
Roland Smith and truck	15.00
Guy Avery	13.60
Robert Mudgett	12.00
Joseph Moulton	10.80
Haven Tibbetts	9.80
Nathaniel Burrows	9.00
Clarence Robinson	6.90
Frank Burrows and truck	6.60
Edwin Elliott	6.40
Henry Tibbetts	4.40
Wallace Nudd	3.20
Walter Nudd	3.20
Lenox Irvine	3.20
William Davison	2.40
Elmer Moody	2.40
Richard Gray	2.00
John Bryant, salt	14.90
William Heard, gravel	2.55

Total		$493.16
Total West District—Highway Account		$2,089.78

GENERAL SNOW REMOVAL

Elmer Thompson, by contract	$2,970.42
Nelson's Garage, erecting snow fence	159.60
Elmer Elliott, land damage	15.00
F. R. Prescott, wire	9.00
Scott Wallace	7.50
Walter Burrows	.40

Total		$3,161.92

GENERAL HIGHWAY EXPENSE

Nelson's Garage	$136.92
State Highway Garage	82.32
C. E. Buzzell, culverts	70.56
Weldon Worthen	62.50
South Tamworth Industries	56.43
Good Roads Machine Corp.	20.21
Ryvers Ainger	16.80

Margaret Slade, watering trough,	
to March, 1939	12.00
Berger Mfg. Co., culverts	9.53
Dora P. Wing, watering trough,	
to March, 1938	3.00
Perley C. Knox	1.05
Walter Burrows	.50
Total	$471.82

SANDWICH FAIR TRUST FUND

(Entries made under General Highway Expense)
(Includes transportation of Road Machines for alteration)

Ralph Peaslee and truck	$36.60
Asa Bryant and truck	20.80
Otis Cook and truck	19.20
John Martin	6.40
Wilbur Mudgett	6.40
Total (Charged to Trust Interest— in hands of Trustees)	$89.40

Total General Highway Expense	$561.22
Total Highways and Bridges	$10,277.76

RECAPITULATION OF
TOWN HIGHWAYS AND BRIDGES

	Maintenance	Bushes	Snow	Sanding	Total	Grand Totals
East	$1,046.70	$331.70	$529.80	$256.36	$2,164.56	
North	1,136.30	329.78	341.15	493.05	2,300.28	
West	1,213.82	326.00	56.80	493.16	2,089.78	
						$6,554.62
General	561.22		3,161.92			3,723.14
Totals	$3,958.04	$987.48	$4,089.67	$1,242.57		$10,277.76

Town Highways appropriation	$7,500.00
Sanding from Blanchard Fund	1,000.00
Bal. of Blanchard Fund	204.31
Sandwich Fair Trust Fund (Int. in hands of Trustees)	112.27
	8,816.58
Excess over appropriations	$1,461.18

HURRICANE

TOWN FUNDS EXPENDED—LABOR, TRUCKS, SUPPLIES
EAST DISTRICT—GEORGE W. VITTUM, AGENT

George Vittum and truck	$349.89
Forest Martel and truck	312.40
Arthur Lewis and truck	202.80
Orrin Tilton and truck	112.80
George W. Vittum, Jr.	110.40
Wilbur Martin	79.80
Archie Palmer	50.60
Daniel Clark	39.55
Thomas Nelson	38.40
Harold Nelson	37.60
Charles Tilton	29.20
Harry Haley	20.80
Wilbur Gilman	20.20
Norman Moulton	19.60
Arnold Robinson	19.60
Herbert Nelson	11.20
Theodore Read	9.60
James Prescott	8.40
Wilfred Stone	6.20
Clifton Goodwin	2.40
Granville Smith	1.60
Sumner B. Clark	.80
William Hurd	.80
South Tamworth Industries—plank	58.63
Herbert Perkins, gravel	18.25
Marshall Vittum, gravel	15.76
Charles Bickford, gravel	1.68
E. Martel, sharpening	1.40
Charles Chase, gravel	.50
Ralph Dodge, sharpening tools	.50

Total	$1,581.36

NORTH DISTRICT—RALPH PEASLEE, AGENT
CLEVELAND WEED IN CHARGE, FRENCH BRIDGE
(Includes Part of French Bridge—See also T.R.A.)

Ralph Q. Peaslee and truck	$391.13
Wilbur Cook and truck	265.80
Cleveland Weed	165.33
Everett Campbell	49.60
Harry Wallace	49.40
William Stone	46.60
John Campbell	44.60
Clifton Campbell	41.60
Irving Mudgett	40.40
Herbert Perkins and truck	41.20

George McCormack	37.40
Fred Barnes	35.80
Albert Brownlie	32.00
Nestor Davis	31.15
Marshall Vittum and truck	30.80
Roger Plummer	29.60
Howard Stevenson	28.80
Edson Worthen	25.20
Louis Vittum	18.60
Edwin Elliott	18.40
Herman Tilton	18.40
Jesse Ambrose and truck	16.80
Stanley Parris	16.40
Robert Penniman	16.00
John Martin	15.20
Eugene Fogg	15.20
William Nixon	14.80
Charles Whitehouse	14.20
Joseph Wilkins	12.80
Elmer Moody	12.00
Paul Townsend	12.00
Nathaniel Burrows	8.64
Clarence Brown	8.40
William Hurd	8.00
Harold Elliott	7.00
W. Leroy White	6.00
Forest Davis	5.62
Arthur Watson	5.62
Joseph Moulton	5.60
John Bryant	4.40
Everett Davey	3.20
South Tamworth Industries, Cement, and Lumber	823.43
Charles Bickford, bridge timbers	202.25
Nelson's Garage	132.75
William J. O'Brien, electric wire	49.00
Lester Moody, gravel	15.20
William Heard, gravel	10.00
Jesse Ambrose, gravel	6.70
Louise Peaslee, dynamite	4.56
Harry Clark, gravel	4.50
Harry Wallace, gravel	4.50
Wilfred Plummer, gravel	4.00
John Bryant, supplies	3.60
Total	$2,910.18

WEST DISTRICT—W. ASA BRYANT, AGENT

W. Asa Bryant and truck	$380.10
Frank Burrows and truck	303.80
Richard Gray and truck	283.80
Guy Avery	136.40
Arthur Lewis and truck	62.60
Clarence Robinson and truck	61.80
Frank Mudgett	60.80
Robert Mudgett	58.40
William English	41.40
Paul Taylor and truck	41.20
Arthur Avery	33.20
Elwood Mudgett	30.20
Roland Jackson	25.80
Francis Mudgett	23.80
Robert Woodward	21.40
Eugene Fogg	20.60
Wilbur Mudgett	19.60
Walter Nudd	18.20
Frank Martin	16.60
Laurence Blumberg	16.30
Harold English	11.80
Norman Hodge	9.60
Harvey Dennis	8.80
Charles Mudgett	7.80
John Martin	6.40
Clarence Plummer	6.40
Herman Tilton	6.40
Richard Gray	6.00
Asahel Wallace	5.60
Clarence Robinson	5.20
Albert Brownlie	4.60
William Mudgett	3.20
Arthur Avery, bridge stringers	16.00
So. Tamworth Industries, plank.	12.30
Wilfred Plummer, gravel	7.50
John Bryant, hardware	.72
E. I. Hamilton, hardware	.38
Total	$1,774.70

HURRICANE GENERAL EXPENSE

C. E. Buzzell, R. C. Pipe	$320.11	
Paid Treas. State of N. H.—		
Excess over T.R.A. (See T.R.A. Summary)	851.97	
Alice Moorhouse, lease	75.00	
Total General		$1,247.08
Total all Districts		$7,513.32
Town App. T.R.A. (See T.R.A. Summary)		820.48
GRAND TOTAL Town Funds expended on HURRICANE		$8,333.80

T.R.A.
RECOMMENDED BY STATE FOR HURRICANE DAMAGE

Appropriated by Town	$820.48
Allocated by State	3,281.91
Excess, paid State, over joint account	851.97
	$4,954.36

Cleveland Weed	407.00
Ralph Q. Peaslee, truck	308.71
Elmer Elliott, team	234.10
Wilbur Quimby	196.75
Jesse L. Ambrose, truck	160.00
George Vittum, Jr.	133.80
Marshall Vittum, truck	133.60
Forrest Martel	120.00
George W. Vittum	117.20
Paul Taylor	115.20
Clarence Robinson, truck	112.80
Harold Elliott	112.70
Charles Shackford	99.37
W. Asa Bryant, truck	89.04
Clarence Brown	78.80
Orrin Tilton and truck	68.00
Theodore Read, truck	63.00
Arthur Lewis, truck	61.20
Wilbur Cook, truck	50.40
Fred Allen	48.15
Fred Barnes	42.50
W. Leroy White	37.00
George McCormack	32.20
Irving Mudgett	30.00
Frank Burrows, truck	28.80
Lyle Grant	22.50
Herbert Nelson	21.80
Herman Tilton	20.60
Richard Gray, truck	19.20
Forest Davis	16.87
Aliston Grant	16.97
Thomas Nelson	16.80
Joseph Moulton	12.45
Asahel Wallace	11.93
Guy Avery	11.80
Arthur Watson	11.25
Nathaniel Burrows, truck	10.40
Kenneth Vittum	8.80
William Vittum	8.80
Harry Wallace	8.40
Wilbur Martin	8.20
Albert Brownlie	7.20
Charles Weed	7.20
Archie Palmer	6.40

Robert Penniman	6.40	
Roger Plummer	6.40	
Daniel Clark	4.60	
Theodore Wallace	4.60	
Clifton Campbell	4.40	
Everett Campbell	4.40	
William English	3.20	
Eugene Fogg	3.20	
John Martin	3.20	
Francis Mudgett	3.20	
Richard Mudgett	3.20	
Scott Wallace	3.20	
	$3,177.79	$3,177.79

SUPPLIES, MATERIALS, EQUIPMENT

C. E. Buzzell, R. Concrete Pipe	$477.46	
South Tamworth Industries	353.83	
Cleveland Weed, equipment	122.75	
Lester Moody, gravel	79.85	
Marshall Vittum, gravel	59.88	
Harry Wallace, gravel	54.75	
W. Asa Bryant, dynamite, etc.	40.25	
Harry Clark, gravel	35.25	
Walter Taylor, gravel	35.10	
Charles Bickford, stone	27.50	
Wilfred Z. Plummer, gravel	25.50	
William Heard, gravel	21.75	
Arthur Avery, gravel	17.10	
Berger Metal Culvert	15.88	
Herbert Perkins, gravel	10.20	
George McCormack, gravel	9.00	
Elizabeth Grant, gravel	6.45	
Robert Penniman, gravel	5.70	
Roy F. Bickford, gravel	5.10	
Lewis Currier, gravel	3.90	
Horace Davis, gravel	3.90	
John Bryant, hardware	3.55	
Jesse L. Ambrose, gravel	2.80	
W. Leroy White, stone	2.00	
Julia P. Lombard, gravel	1.80	
John Woodbridge	1.75	
	$1,423.00	$1,423.00

TAYLOR BRIDGE (WEST ABUTMENT)

Cleveland Weed—by bid Labor	$110.13	
Materials	174.87	
	$285.00	$285.00

State Balance Sheet—
 J. F. Chick—Cement $67.32
     Delivery 1.25

         · $68.57 $68.57

  Total Expenditures under T.R.A. $4,954.36·

STATE ESTIMATE OF HURRICANE DAMAGE
AND
HURRICANE SUMMARY

Estimate of Hurricane Damage in survey
 made by State Engineers and Town Road
 Agents, Oct. 10, 1938—
  Washouts $15,815.00
  Culverts   1,620.00
  Bridges   9,775.00

  Estimated Total Hurricane Damage $27,210.00
Total expenditures on Town Ledger for
 Hurricane, including Quimby trustee gift of
 $1,000.00 for bridge and Town T.R.A.
 contribution, but less excess T.R.A. paid to
 State ($851.97—see below) $6,661.35
  T.R.A. Appropriation $820.48
  Excess T.R.A. paid State 851.97

  Total Town contribution to
   T.R.A.   1,672.45

  Total Town Ledger,
   Hurricane $8,333.80
State allotment T.R.A.   3,281.90
Project #2004,
 W.P.A. Labor $3,913.39
Project #2004,
 W.P.A. trucks 667.52

  Total W.P.A. $4,580.91

Total Town, State and Government funds
 expended on Hurricane $16,196.61
Revised Estimate:
 Estimated expenditure necessary
  to bring condition of highways,
  culverts, and bridges to same
  condition as before Hurricane:
    $6,000.00

NOTCH AND DALE ROAD (Legislative Special)
G. Roland Smith, Agent

Town Appropriation	$500.00	
State Allotment	750.00	
Total available		$1,250.00
G. Roland Smith and truck	$578.80	
Fred Crowell	219.20	
S. Maurice Smith	66.00	
James Beede	35.60	
Irving Gray	34.80	
Harold English	30.40	
Fred Mudgett	22.80	
Robert Woodward	16.00	
Robert Berry	11.60	
Wilbur Martin	10.00	
Walter Taylor	9.60	
Lawrence Blumberg	5.20	
Kenneth Irvine	5.20	
So. Tamworth Industries	1.58	
E. I. Hamilton	.84	
N. E. Metal Culvert Co.	183.64	
Highway Garage	7.13	
Total	$1,238.39	
Credit Town Balance $4.64 plus		
State Balance $6.97	11.61	
Total		$1,250.00
Library—		
Mabel E. Ambrose, Treas.		$493.50
Charities—		
Old Age Assistance		
Carroll County	$268.80	
State of New Hampshire	414.93	
		683.73
Town Poor		
Margaret Fish,		
Supplies for Edwin Fogg	200.00	
F. A. Bickford,		
Hauling wood for Edwin Fogg	7.00	
Ross M. Graves,		
Camp and stove for Edwin Fogg	50.00	
Lease of land for Edwin Fogg	10.00	
Moving Edwin Fogg	8.00	
Eva Mudgett,		
Board of Eva Smith	210.00	

C. J. Goodwin,
 Care of C. S. Ethridge   182.60
Dr. R. H. Thompson,
 Care of C. S. Ethridge   8.00
Glenn Smith,
 Supplies for Harold Denney 9.95
 Supplies for Robert Mudgett 10.00
 Supplies for Daniel S. Watson 4.68
 Supplies for Clarence Robinson 27.72
 Supplies for David Glover 192.07
E. I. Hamilton,
 Supplies for David Glover 3.90
 Clothing, Clarence Robinson 8.80
Dr. F. S. Lovering,
 Glasses for David Glover 7.75
Arnall's Trading Post,
 Clothing for David Glover 4.79
Theodore Wallace,
 Sawing wood for David Glover 3.20
Carroll County Home,
 For Hattie Tappan   368.28
Grace S. Ford,
 For Albert Percival   14.29
G. R. Smith,
 Sawing wood for A. Brownlie 1.50
Clarence E. Cole,
 For C. S. Ethridge record .28

            1,332.81

County Poor
 Margaret Fish,
  Groceries for V. L. Whiting * 5.00
 Glenn Smith,
  Groceries for Roland Summers 7.06
 E. I. Hamilton,
  Groceries for Wilfred Sturgeon 5.24
  Supplies George Scriggins .75
 C. J. Goodwin,
  Board, etc., for George Scriggins 155.02
 Robert S. Quinby, M.D.
  Med. exam. of J. J. Sullivan 5.00
 Grace S. Ford,
  Board of J. J. Sullivan 50.00

            $228.07

* Repaid to Town

PATRIOTIC PURPOSES

Memorial Day and Other Celebrations—
Memorial Day
William H. Forristall	$109.10

Old Home Week
James H. Beede, Treas.	150.00

Christmas
Arnall's Trading Post, bulbs	6.00

	$265.10

Soldiers' Aid
Case I, Robert S. Quinby, M.D.	
Professional services	95.50
Case II, Laconia Hospital	49.25

	144.75

Projects
Wood Cutting Project #1460
Glenn Smith, supplies	3.30
John W. Bryant, supplies	2.69
G. R. Smith, hauling wood	1.00
Ralph Q. Peaslee, filing saws	1.50
Paul W. Taylor, yarding wood	13.00
A. D. Hamilton, yarding wood	61.00

	82.49

W.P.A. PROJECT #1404 (WIDENING ROADS)

Trucks—
Frank Burrows, truck	$243.20
Nathaniel Burrows, truck	99.20
Ralph Q. Peaslee, truck	54.50
Arthur Lewis, truck	31.20

	428.10

Labor—
Frank Burrows, foreman	93.28
W. Asa Bryant	4.00
Fred Barnes	5.60
Elwood Mudgett	5.60
Scott Wallace	5.60

	114.08

Tools and Supplies—
Glenn Smith	19.69
John Bryant	12.85
William J. O'Brien	11.87
E. I. Hamilton	6.50
Ralph Q. Peaslee	4.05
Ralph Dodge	2.45

Sandwich General Store	1.00	
John Bryant, Dynamite Caps	86.34	
Weeks & Smith, Dynamite Caps	22.00	
William Nelson,		
Use of Compressor Drill	300.00	
		466.75
Total		$1,008.93
Appropriated by Town to		
match projects	$1,000.00	
Overdraft	8.93	
		$1,008.93
Payroll paid by Federal funds	$2,752.16	

UNCLASSIFIED

Lakes Region Association, Appropriation		128.00
Taxes Bought by Town		
J. Frank Atwood	62.28	
Jennie Avery	78.38	
Mildred McCrea	7.88	
Wallace Nudd	29.62	
Marjorie V. Sargent	53.82	
Henry H. Bennett	5.88	
Mathew M. Blunt	3.06	
Mary A. Flood	31.26	
Forest Products Co.	45.36	
		$317.54

DISCOUNTS AND ABATEMENTS

Fred Boyd, address unknown	$2.00
Fred N. Burrows, Error of assessment	5.64
George O. Cook, over 70	2.00
Charles S. Cram, adjustment	.57
Elizabeth Crockett, over 70	2.00
Everett Davey, under 21	2.00
Minnie L. Demick, deceased	2.00
Harvey O. Dennis, discharged veteran	2.00
Pauline E. Dennis	2.00
Harold Denny, unable to pay	2.00
Alice Denny, unable to pay	2.00
Est. of Nellie F. Eastman, error	33.84
George L. Eaton, over 70	2.00
Harry O. Haley,	
by order of Selectmen	69.65
Adelaide J. Marston	2.00
Dorothy M. Martin,	
Paid in Manchester	2.00
Clifford Mathews, left town	2.00

Marjorie Mathews, left town	2.00
Jesse A. Mudgett	2.56
Jennie E. Mudgett	2.00
Grace LaCroix Ogden	2.00
Helen Pettengill,	
Paid in Meredith	2.00
Grace Plume, left town	2.00
George Scriggins, over 70	2.00
Eva G. Smith	2.00
Elizabeth Weed, resident in Mass.	2.00
Edson W. Worthen	2.00
Weldon W. Worthen	4.82
Heirs of George A. Collins, adjustment	1.41
Rev. Edward R. Welles,	
Error in assessment	31.02
Hale House Association,	
Error in Warrant	84.60

278.11

Interest	
Meredith Village Savings Bank	63.25

NEW CONSTRUCTION AND IMPROVEMENT
SQUAM LAKE ROAD
SANDWICH S.A.M.C. SPECIAL
NEW CONSTRUCTION AND PERMANENT IMPROVEMENTS

Town Contribution	$1,999.89	
State Allotment	1,999.88	
Total Expenditure, Joint Account		$3,999.77
Ross Graves	$453.00	
Ryvers Ainger	252.00	
Clarence Graves	247.20	
Fred Mudgett	189.60	
Roland Jackson	180.00	
Lewis Elliott	126.40	
Edson Taylor	118.80	
Orris Littlefield	115.60	
Ernest McDonald	115.20	
Fred Babb	108.80	
George Brown	108.80	
Jerry Martin	102.40	
Charles Mudgett	98.80	
Clarence Plummer	98.80	
Newell Burrows	80.00	
Fred Hodgdon	80.00	
Wilfred Sturgeon	76.80	
Harold Denney	73.20	
William Nelson	70.00	
John Callahan	63.20	
Edwin Elliott	63.20	

Irving Gray	63.20	
James Prescott	60.00	
Thomas Nelson	56.00	
Edson Worthen	49.60	
Daniel Clark	41.20	
Theodore Wallace	32.00	
Scott Wallace	31.60	
Asahel Wallace	28.40	
Francis Mudgett	14.00	
Robert Mudgett	7.20	
Earl Dearborn	3.60	
Lester Burrows	3.20	
Total Labor		3,211.80
State of N. H., Tar	285.25	
State of N. H., R. C. Pipe	201.55	
William Heard, Gravel	205.70	
Weeks & Smith, Dynamite	55.60	
Nelson's Garage, Equipment	29.75	
South Tamworth Industries	10.12	
Total Materials		787.97

Total Expended Joint Account		$3,999.77
Treasurer State of New Hampshire		$1,999.89

Waterholes

H. L. Perkins, fence and cartage	4.40
Otis Cook, moving stones	9.20
Fred A. Bickford, moving stones	23.00

	36.60

MOSES HALL FUND—W. ASA BRYANT, AGENT

(Completion of State Aid on Mt. Israel Road Between Diamond Ledge and Dale Roads)

W. Asa Bryant and truck	$168.35
Guy Avery	53.00
Frank Mudgett	40.20
Charles Mudgett	35.20
Otis Cook and truck	33.00
Clarence Robinson and truck	28.80
Frank Burrows and truck	24.60
Henry Boyle	22.40
Elwood Mudgett	22.40
Paul Taylor and truck	22.20
Eugene Fogg	21.00
Ryvers Ainger and truck	15.40
Richard Gray and truck	15.00
Ryvers Ainger, truck and man	14.40
Robert Woodward	12.80
Otis Cook, labor	10.40

Arthur Lewis	8.00	
Richard Gray, labor	6.60	
Edson Worthen	2.40	
State Highway Dept.—culverts	195.20	
Richard Gray, hard-pan	5.25	
Arthur Lewis, gravel	1.95	
Ralph Dodge, sharpening tools	1.30	
Glenn Smith, cord	.38	
	$760.23	
Paid Mabel I. Quimby (Annuity)	200.00	
Total		960.23
Refund—Credit by double entry to Ryvers Ainger ($14.40)		
Total Hall Fund Received payment of Hall Fund By Trustees to Town	$899.97	
Balance Hall Fund in hands of Treasurer, Jan. 31, 1938	107.90	
Total	$1,007.87	
Hall Fund Balance in hands of Treasurer, Jan. 31, 1939	62.04	
	$945.83	
Total Outlay		2,996.72
Indebtedness		
Payments on Temporary Loans Meredith Village Savings Bank	3,000.00	
Refunds		
William Heard, Tr. overpayment	8.66	
		3,008.66
Payments to Other Governmental Divisions		
Taxes paid to State	2,940.00	
Taxes paid to County	7,922.00	
Payments to School Districts		

Appropriations	$12,581.00		
Dog Licenses	221.08		
School Fund Note	133.92		
Total for Schools		12,936.00	
			23,798.00
Total Payments for All Purposes			58,280.94
Cash on Hand Jan. 31, 1939			2,635.92
Grand Total			$60,916.86

REPORT OF THE TRUST FUNDS OF THE TOWN OF SANDWICH, N. H., ON JULY 31, 1939.

Date of Creation	TRUST FUNDS—PURPOSE OF CREATION	How Invested	Amount of Principal	Rate of Interest	Balance of Income on hand at Beginning of Year	Income During Year	Expended During Year	Balance of Income on Hand at End of Year
Feb. 20, 1908	William Elgh, Cary Fund	New Hampshire Savings Bank	$107.43	2½	$25.45	$3.30	$5.00	$23.75
Feb. 8, 1910	villa P. Worroll, Cary uFd	New Hampshire Savings Bank	210.55	2½	5.30	5.38	5.50	5.18
Feb. 8, 1910	Cary Fund	New Hampshire Savings Bank	100.00	2½	3.03	2.53	3.03	2.53
Dec. 31, 1910	Susan Sherman, Cary Fund	New Hampshire Savings Bank	150.00	2½	4.54	3.78	4.54	3.78
Dec. 8, 1911	Samuel Chase, Cary uFd	New Hampshire Savings Bank	50.00	2½	1.51	1.26	1.51	1.26
Dec. 8, 1911	Alfred A. Marston, Cary Fund	New Hampshire Savings Bank	500.00	2½	82.17	14.40	12.00	84.57
April 27, 1914	Ella B. Ad	New Hampshire Savings Bank	25.00	2½	2.16	.68		2.84
Nov. 24, 1914	Mrs Mudgett, Cary uFd	New Hampshire Savings Bank	25.00	2½	.75	.63	.75	.63
Jan. 27, 1917	Mrs. Henry Hanson, Cary uFd	New Hampshire Savings Bank	25.00	2½	.75	.63	.75	.63
Jan. 3, 1916	Mrs H. Wie, Cary Fund	Mrs Savings Bank	1,000.00	3	960.18	58.46	68.66	949.98
Feb. 14, 1917	Mrs. Mary Peaslee, Cary uFd	New Hampshire Savings Bank	100.00	2½	3.48		3.48	
Feb. 14, 1917	Nellie J. Dbl, Cary Fund	New Hampshire Savings Bank	100.00	2½	3.03	2.53	3.03	2.53
Feb. 4, 1918	Mrs. Emma Gx, Cary uFd	New Hampshire Savings Bank	25.00	2½	.75	.63	.75	.63
Feb. 4, 1918	Mrs Mr, Cary uFd	New Hampshire Savings Bank	100.00	2½		2.50	2.50	
Aug. 23, 1920	Ann D. George, Cary Fund	New Hampshire Savings Bank	150.40	2½	63.08	5.33		68.41
Aug. 16, 192	Charles W. Donovan, Cary uFd	New Hampshire Savings Bk	100.00	2½	1.46	2.53		3.99
Mar. 25, 191	Walter D. Hill, Cary Fund	New Hampshire Savings Bank	200.00	2½	23.67	5.58		29.25
June 7, 192	William B. Fellows, Cary uFd	New Hampshire Savings uFd	100.00	2½	26.56	3.11	3.00	26.67
June 7, 192	I. Hartwell Smith, Cary Fund	New Hampshire Savings Bank	80.00	2½	3.96	2.04	2.45	3.55
Nov. 4, 192	Me Hodge, Cary uFd	New Hampshire Savings Bank	25.00	2½	.75	.63	.75	.63
Feb. 7, 193	Ga A. Gilman, Jn, Cary Fund	New Hampshire Savings Bank	40.00	2½	1.21	1.01	1.21	1.01
Feb. 2, 191	George W. Jn and Julia Tappan, Cary	New Hampshire Savings Bank	220.00	2½	58.69	6.90	4.00	61.59
Dec. 30, 1912	Fund Erastus P. wl, Library Fund	New Hampshire Savings Bank	100.00	2½	3.03	2.53	3.03	2.53
Feb. 8, 1924	Elizabeth H. dk, Cary uFd	New Hampshire Savings Bank	500.00	2½		12.53	12.53	
May 8, 196	Ora Fellows, Cary Fund	ag Savings Bank	100.00	3	3.34	3.11	6.45	
June 8, 196	Hamlin Huntress, Hd	rhg Savings Bank	50.00	3	1.51	1.51	1.51	1.51
June 8, 1927	Charlotte Wallace, Cary uFd	Mg Savings Bank	200.00	3	6.05	6.23		12.28
July 19, 197	Edwin Mn, Cary Fund	Amoskeag Savings Bank	50.00	3	.60	1.50	1.50	.62
Feb. 2, 191	Bessie Lovering, Cary uFd	Amoskeag Savings Bank	25.00	3	.76	.77		1.53

Date	Fund / Account	Where Deposited	Amount
Dec. 29, 1931	Herman E. Lewis, Cemetery Fund	Amoskeag Savings Bank	.76
June 16, 1923	Mabel Sturgis, School Fund	Amoskeag Savings Bank	.76
Feb. 2, 1928	Melissa G. Rowe, Cemetery Fund	Amoskeag Savings Bank	93.54
Feb. 2, 1928	Huldah Ann Wiggin, Cemetery Fund	Meredith Village Savings Bank	3.04
July 26, 1928	A. B. Hoag, Cemetery Fund	Meredith Village Savings Bank	
Aug. 6, 1928	Stella A. Quimby, Cemetery Fund	Meredith Village Savings Bank	20.97
Nov. 24, 1928	George L. Clark, Cemetery Fund	Meredith Village Savings Bank	
Aug. 12, 1929	Mabel Quimby and Mary Leavens, Cemetery Fund	Meredith Village Savings Bank	120.73
Nov. 24, 1928	Freewill Baptist Church, Cemetery Fund	Meredith Village Savings Bank	.....
Jan. 17, 1933	Arven Blanchard, Cemetery Fund	Meredith Village Savings Bank	.....
July 27, 1936	Asahel Wallace Cemetery Fund	Meredith Village Savings Bank	5.34
Aug. 27, 1936	George S. Hoyt Cemetery Fund	Meredith Village Savings Bank	9.19
May 1, 1920	Charles Blanchard, Library Fund	Meredith Village Savings Bank	10.76
May 1, 1920	Charles Blanchard, Highway Fund	Government Bonds	.....
May 1, 1920	Charles Blanchard, Highway Fund	Government and Municipal Bonds	.....
May 1, 1920	Charles Blanchard, Highway Fund	Amoskeag Savings Bank	.....
July 11, 1928	Charles Blanchard, Highway Fund	New Hampshire Savings Bank	6.00
Nov. 3, 1934	Charles Blanchard, Highway Fund	Meredith Savings Bank	189.13
May 1, 1934	Charles Blanchard, Highway Fund	Peoples Savings Bank, Manchester. Liquidated and transferred to Amoskeag Savings Bank	.....
Nov. 1, 1933	Charles Blanchard, Highway Fund	Manchester Savings Bank	.....
Jan. 31, 1918	School Fund, Note for Schools	Town of Sandwich	62.00
Sept. 28, 1933	Frank B. Watson, Cemetery Fund	2 U. S. 3% Bonds, $100 each	.....
Jan. 31, 1931	Moses A. Hall, Highway Fund	City Savings Bank, Laconia	.....
Jan. 1, 1931	Moses A. Hall, Highway Fund	Plymouth Guaranty Savings Bank	.....
Jan. 1, 1931	Moses A. Hall, Highway Fund	Merrimack River Savings Bank (In hands of Receiver)	.....
Jan. 1, 1931	Moses A. Hall, Highway Fund	Laconia Savings Bank	.....
Jan. 1, 1931	Moses A. Hall, Highway Fund	Stratford Savings Bank transferred to Manchester Savings Bank, Jan. 29, 1939	.....
Jan. 1, 1931	Moses A. Hall, Highway Fund	Merrimac County Savings Bank	85.82
Jan. 1, 1931	Moses A. Hall, Highway Fund	Manchester Savings Bank	137.34
Jan. 1, 1931	Moses A. Hall, Highway Fund	New Hampshire Savings Bank	140.55
Jan. 1, 1931	Moses A. Hall, Highway Fund	Amoskeag Savings Bank	113.64
Feb. 16, 1937	Town of Sandwich, Town Fair Fund	Manchester Savings Bank	38.48
July 1, 1937	Daniel D. Atwood, School Fund	Amoskeag Savings Bank	112.27
July 1, 1937	Daniel D. Atwood, Sidewalk Fund	Peoples Savings Bank, Manchester. Liquidated and transferred to Amoskeag Savings Bank, Sep. 27, 1938	182.70 / 18.20
Aug. 2, 1937	Daniel D. Atwood, Cemetery Fund	Meredith Village Savings Bank	6.07
Aug. 16, 1937	Edmund Quimby, Cemetery Fund	Meredith Village Savings Bank	
May 3, 1938	William McClosky, Cemetery Fund	Meredith Village Savings Bank	1.00
Oct. 20, 1938	Nathaniel Burleigh Cemetery Fund	Meredith Village Savings Bank	1.00

$2,669.48

Auditor's Report

We, the auditors of the Town of Sandwich, have examined the accounts of the Selectmen, Road Agents, Treasurers of the Library Trustees, of Veterans' Association, of Old Home Week Association, of the Trustees of Trust Funds and Town Clerk, Perley C. Knox, and found them correct and properly vouched and in the hands of Mabel E. Ambrose, Treasurer of Library Trustees, $235.26 on deposit in Meredith Trust Company; in the hands of Beatrice Burrows at Library $5.06 in cash; in the hands of William Forristall, Treasurer of Veterans' Association, none in cash; in the hands of James H. Beede, Treasurer of Old Home Week Association, $.63 on deposit in Meredith Trust Company; in the hands of William Heard, Treasurer of Trustees of Trust Funds, an unexpended income amounting to $2,669.48 in various Savings Banks, and trust fund principals amounting to $83,777.83 in bonds and bank deposits; in the hands of James H. Beede, Treasurer of the Town, a total of $2,-635.92 in cash and on deposit, and no cash in the hands of Perley C. Knox, Town Clerk; in the hands of Ryvers F. Ainger, Fire Chief, $358.15.

ALISTON H. GRANT,
H. W. CLARK
CLEVELAND WEED,
Auditors of Town of Sandwich.

Feb. 18, 1939

Wentworth Library

RECEIPTS

Balance on hand, Jan. 31, 1938	$218.69	
Cash on hand	.98	
Cash on hand at Library Jan. 31, 1938	1.00	
		$220.67
Town Appropriation by vote	420.00	
Town Appropriation, by Law	73.50	
Blanchard Fund	170.00	
Jewell Fund for 1937	15.00	
Receipts at Library	17.25	
		695.75
		$916.42

PAYMENTS

White Mountain Power Co.	$23.68
Geo. O. Cook, janitor	63.00
Cecil Talbott, janitor	46.80
Cecil Talbott, work on wood	4.00
Doris Chittick, 2 Feb. Openings	4.00
Beatrice Burrows, salary	228.00
Beatrice Burrows, July and August Monday Openings	27.00
Beatrice Burrows, Summer School	18.00
Beatrice Burrows, Transportation	2.50
Ethel Atwood, Asst. Librarian	60.60
Ethel Atwood, 13 hours' work	3.90
Magazines	19.25
Arthur T. White, Magazines	30.75
New England News and Wormrath Bookshop, New Books	41.68
Beatrice Burrows, Supplies	1.52
Wm. Forristal, Supplies	2.50
H. W. Wilson, Catalogue Book	2.75
Stamps and Stationery	1.48
Service Charges for year	4.50
Daniel Clark, 13 hours' work, cleaning after hurricane	5.20
Perley C. Knox, work on grounds, and bag of fertilizer	17.30
2 cords wood	13.00
Jesse L. Ambrose, 1⅛ cords heavy wood	9.00
Fred Bickford, 7 cords wood	32.50
Incidental expenses at Library	13.19

Total Expenses for year	$676.10
Balance on hand in checking account Jan. 31, 1939	235.26
Cash on hand at Library Jan. 31, 1939	5.06
	$916.42

MABEL E. AMBROSE,
Treasurer.

Grateful thanks are extended to
  The Quimby Trustees
  Mrs. Mary Coolidge
  Mrs. T. Guthrie Speers
  Mrs. Carl Beede
  Miss Doris Benz
  Miss Jessy Flanigen
  and many others for their generous gifts of money and Books.

Old Home Week Association

RECEIPTS

Balance from 1937	$17.86
Appropriation 1938	150.00
Stuart W. Heard, refund	.60

$168.46

EXPENDITURES

Alice M. Moorhouse, printing	$30.00
Stuart W. Heard, sports	20.00
Chester H. Howe, Sunday Service	5.00
Edward R. Welles, Sunday Service	5.00
Leon J. Manville, band	50.00
Vera Presby, postage	5.01
Jean Stevens, reception	8.32
Joseph Wentworth, entertainment	43.00
Bank charges	1.50
Cash on hand, Jan. 31, 1939	.63

$168.46

JAMES H. BEEDE, *Treasurer.*

Sandwich Veterans Association

RECEIPTS

Appropriation for 1938	$75.00
Balance from 1937	38.69
	$113.69

EXPENDITURES

Rochester City Band	$50.00
Ladies' Aid, for suppers	25.00
G. E. Rundlett, flags	11.10
Francis Buffum, speaker	10.00
Albert C. Gale, placing flags, East and West	5.00
Alice Smith, filling 48 baskets	3.00
E. D. Fitts, filling 18 baskets	2.00
David Glover, placing flags, West	2.00
Guy B. Thompson, 60 pansy baskets	1.00
	$109.10

Balance on hand Executor of Late Col.
Charles B. Hoyt $4.59

WM. H. FORRISTALL,
Chairman.

May 30, 1938.

BLISTER RUST STATEMENT
1938
TOWN OF SANDWICH

Town Program—
Crew cost	$99.58	
Foreman cost	25.00	
Total expended		$124.58
Received from Town	100.00	
Expended from town funds	99.58	
Balance due Town		.42
Area covered		280 acres
Currant and gooseberry bushes destroyed		1,406
Number of local men employed		9

SANDWICH CHAPTER OF THE
AMERICAN RED CROSS
1939

Again the chief activities of this chapter for the past year have been the raising of funds for Relief at the request of the National Red Cross—for the Chinese War Sufferers, but especially for the Hurricane Disaster of last September; once more the people of Sandwich were very generous. Through the efforts of the local chapter reimbursement to the extent of about $60 for damage to a Sandwich dwelling came from National Headquarters from a fund used for rehabilitation at that time.

Another Dental Clinic was sponsored during the winter; there is to be one this winter, and we hope every winter. It was voted to give $5.00 toward hot school lunches; a quantity of cod liver oil was furnished Miss Nelson for distribution among the children of Sandwich. Eye examination and glasses, four tonsil operations, also two dental plates for a fire sufferer were paid for. Your membership in the Sandwich chapter helps with this work.

IDA L. ROGERS, *Secretary.*

SANDWICH CHAPTER
AMERICAN RED CROSS—1938
BRANCHES: CENTER HARBOR, MOULTONBORO

RECEIPTS

Balance on hand Jan. 1938		$451.56
For cod liver oil		6.60
Rockingham Park Charity Fund		25.00
Collections for Chinese war sufferers		38.07
First Prize, Sandwich Fair, Miss Nelson		8.00
For N. E. and N. Y. Hurricane and Flood Relief:		
Sandwich	$175.40	
Center Harbor	50.00	
Moultonboro	8.00	
		233.40
1938-1939 Roll Call for memberships—		
Sandwich, 81 members		
76 annual	$76.00	
5 contributing	25.00	
Sandwich contributions	54.00	
Center Harbor 58 members	29.00	
		184.00
Total Receipts		$946.63

EXPENSES

Clothing for needy family	8.75
Eye examination and glasses	15.00
School lunches	5.00
Cod liver oil	21.10
To National Headquarters for Chinese Relief	38.07
Dental Clinic	41.50
For fire victim, set of teeth	40.00
Four tonsil cases	40.00
N. E. and N. Y. Hurricane and Flood Relief	233.40
1939 Roll Call—to National Headquarters	69.50
Charge for bank account (5 months)	2.50
Total Expenses	$514.82
Balance by cash on hand	431.81
	$946.63

Cash on hand Jan. 1939		
Meredith Trust Company	$165.83	
Emergency Relief Fund in		
Meredith Village Savings Bank	265.98	
		431.81

ANNA L. COOLIDGE, *Treasurer.*

THE STATE OF NEW HAMPSHIRE

To the Inhabitants of the School district in the town of Sandwich qualified to vote in district affairs:

You are hereby notified to meet at the Town Hall in said district on the eleventh day of March, 1939, at two o'clock in the afternoon, to act upon the following subjects:

1. To choose a Moderator for the coming year.

2. To choose a Clerk for the ensuing year.

3. To choose a Member of the School Board for the ensuing three years.

4. To choose a Treasurer for the ensuing year.

5. To determine and appoint the salaries of the School Board and Truant Officer, and fix the compensation of any other officers or agent of the district.

6. To hear the reports of Agents, Auditors, Committees, or Officers chosen, and pass any vote relating thereto.

7. To choose Agents, Auditors and Committees in relation to any subject embraced in this warrant.

8. To see if the district will vote to make any alteration in the amount of money required to be assessed for the ensuing year for the support of public schools and the payment of the statutory obligations of the district, as determined by the school board in its annual report.

9. To see if the district will vote to provide drainage for the playground at the Center School, and raise and appropriate money for the same.

10. To see if the district will vote to authorize the school board, at its discretion, to assist in providing transportation for children who live within the legal limit of two miles from school, and raise and appropriate the sum of $250 for this purpose.

11. To transact any business that may legally come before said meeting.

Given under our hands at said Sandwich this 20th day of February, 1939.

ALICE D. SMITH,
ALISTON H. GRANT,
GRACE E. AINGER,
School Board.

Report of School Board

We, the School Board of the District of Sandwich, hereby submit the following report for the year beginning July 1, 1937, and ending June 30, 1938.

Amount raised at District Meeting for the support of elementary schools, aside from statutory requirements	$9,241.00	
Salaries of district officers	187.00	
Superintendent's excess salary	290.00	
Truant officer and school census	30.00	
Expenses of administration	50.00	
High school tuition	1,800.00	
Alteration of old buildings	300.00	
New equipment	150.00	
Per capita tax	322.00	
Dog tax	231.04	
School Fund note	133.92	
Equalization Fund for elementary schools	140.34	
Smith Hughes and George Reed Fund	1,014.60	
Total receipts		$13,889.90
Cash on hand July 1, 1937		541.45
Grand total		$14,431.35

PAYMENTS

Salaries of district officers	$187.00
Superintendent's excess salary	314.67
Truant officers and school census	30.00
Expenses of administration	61.00
Teachers' salaries	5,266.30
Text books	188.18
Scholars' supplies	158.88
Other expenses of instruction	204.02
Janitor service	246.00
Fuel	249.80

Light and janitors' supplies	130.27
Minor repairs and expenses	173.37
Medical inspection	44.20
Transportation of pupils	2,120.40
High school tuition	1,620.00
Other special activities	94.42
Per capita tax	322.00
Insurance and bonding	15.00
Alterations of old buildings	138.65
New equipment	35.80
Smith Hughes and George Reed Fund	1,014.60
School nurse	251.39
Lands and new buildings	70.78
Measuring roads	4.50
Appropriation special	462.55

Total payments for all purposes	$13,403.78
Total cash on hand at end of year, June 30, 1937	1,027.57
Grand total	$14,431.35

This is to certify that I have examined the accounts of the School District of Sandwich and found them correct.

SUMNER B. CLARK, *Auditor.*

The above is a report of the receipts and payments of the last fiscal year, beginning July 1, 1937, and ending June 30, 1938, of the Sandwich School District, and is in accordance with the State Law.

Following is a detailed report of expenditures:

SALARIES OF DISTRICT OFFICERS

Grace Ainger	$60.00
Alice D. Smith	50.00
Alistou H. Grant	50.00
Ida Rogers	25.00
William Heard	2.00
	$187.00

SUPERINTENDENT'S EXCESS SALARY

Paid to State Treasurer	$314.67

TRUANT OFFICER AND SCHOOL CENSUS

John S. Quimby $30.00

EXPENSES OF ADMINISTRATION

Louise Brock	$28.00
Ida L. Rogers	10.63
F. W. Jackson	10.51
Almon Bushnell	10.21
Edson C. Eastman	.70
Alice Smith	.60
Eva Nelson	.35

$61.00

TEACHERS' SALARIES

Glorie Mason	$925.00
Jeanne Smith	925.00
Rosealie Burrows	875.00
Helen Weed	875.00
Zellene Young	825.00
Leonard Smith	702.37
Agnes Mooney	138.93

$5,266.30

TEXT BOOKS

Ginn & Co.	$95.51
Webster Publishing Co.	43.29
The John C. Winston Co.	24.98
Beckley Cardy Co.	10.08
Young America	9.30
Silver Burdett Co.	2.57
The Macmillan Co.	1.62
Houghton & Mifflin Co.	.83

$188.18

SCHOLARS' SUPPLIES

Edward E. Babb Co.	$80.39
The Paper Crafters	22.64
The Macmillan Co.	9.90
Almon W. Bushnell	9.00
World Book Co.	8.19
Milton Bradley Co.	7.67
Ginn & Co.	6.95
Educational Test Bureau	4.51
John S. Cheever Co.	3.30

Houghton Mifflin	1.80
Philip H. James	1.52
J. L. Hammett Co.	1.05
Lardlaw Bros.	1.01
Bureau of Publication	.95

$158.88

OTHER EXPENSES OF INSTRUCTION

T. E. Compton	$142.52
F. W. Jackson	22.89
Edward E. Babb Co.	9.26
Houghton Mifflin Co.	8.35
South Tamworth Industries	6.85
O. H. Toothaker	6.12
William H. Forristall	3.75
Rosealie Burrows	1.75
Glorie Mason	1.00
Alice Smith	.93
The Meredith News	.60

$204.02

JANITOR SERVICE

Wallace Nudd	$95.00
Kenneth Vittum	38.00
Stewart Bryant	38.00
Rosealie Burrows (work done by children)	38.00
Richard Elliott	37.00

$246.00

FUEL

Otis Cook	$68.00
Harold Elliott	55.25
Elisha Mudgett	47.50
Herbert Perkins	45.00
Roland Smith	15.20
Kenneth Vittum	4.80
Lester Burrows, Jr.	3.50
Clarence Robinson	3.20
South Tamworth Industries	3.00
Newel Burrows	2.60
Wilbur Martin	1.75

$249.80

LIGHT AND JANITOR'S SUPPLIES

Public Service Co. of N. H.	$48.88
Edward E. Babb & Co.	38.05
White Mountain Power Co.	21.60
Cheshire Chemical Co.	15.00
Procter & Gamble	4.00
Weeks & Smith	1.70
Glenn Smith	.49
John Bryant	.35
Arnall's Trading Post	.20

$130.27

MINOR REPAIRS AND EXPENSES

Mrs. Eva Mudgett	$23.80
Edward E. Babb & Co.	16.91
Severance Bryant	16.29
John Bryant	15.00
Wilbur Martin	14.64
South Tamworth Industries	11.21
Wallace Nudd	9.46
Evelena Fitts	9.25
Norman Hodge	9.00
Harriette Robinson	7.30
Sydney Elliott	6.00
A. Flanagan	5.76
Grant Hodsdon	4.25
Clarence Robinson	4.00
Alistou Grant	3.00
Eugene Wallace	2.50
Delphine Campbell	2.50
E. J. Dearborn	2.26
Sumner B. Clark	2.20
Glenn Smith	1.97
F. R. Prescott	1.58
Herbert Perkins	1.50
Perley Knox	1.24
Harold Elliott	1.00
Rosealie Burrows	.75

$173.37

MEDICAL INSPECTION

Dr. R. H. Thompson	$42.00
Eva Nelson	2.20

$44.20

TRANSPORTATION

Mrs. Hazel Hurd	$429.60	
Mrs. Philomene Lewis	309.70	
W. J. O'Brien	271.50	
Jesse Mudgett	271.50	
Mrs. May Plummer	268.50	
Leon Smith	222.80	
Eric Ingles	206.40	
Harry Haley	140.40	
		$2,120.40

HIGH SCHOOL TUITION

Trustees Alfred Quimby Fund	$1,620.00

OTHER SPECIAL ACTIVITIES

Roland Smith	$74.40	
Ralph Peaslee	13.60	
Walter Burrows	4.92	
Herbert Perkins	1.50	
		$94.42

INSURANCE AND BONDING

Clyde B. Foss	$15.00

OTHER FIXED CHARGES

State Treasurer (per capita)	$322.00

LANDS AND NEW BUILDINGS

Edyth N. Weed	$50.00	
W. L. White	16.28	
Sumner B. Clark	4.50	
		$70.78

ALTERATIONS OF OLD BUILDINGS

John Bryant	$81.40	
Wallace Nudd	38.22	
J. A. Sullivan	19.03	
		$138.65

New Equipment

J. L. Hammett	20.50
F. W. Jackson	7.00
Sears, Roebuck Co.	4.30
Procter & Gamble	4.00

$35.80

Measuring Road

Sumner B. Clark $4.50

Federal Aid

Smith Hughes Fund	$800.29
Paid to Quimby Trustees	
George Reed Fund	214.31
Paid to Quimby Trustees	

$1,014.60

Nurse

Eva Nelson $251.39

Special Appropriation

Severance Bryant	$218.32
South Tamworth Industries	191.63
Herbert Perkins	37.60
George Vittum	15.00

$462.55

ALICE D. SMITH,
ALISTON H. GRANT,
GRACE E. AINGER,
School Board of Sandwich.

SCHOOL BOARD'S BUDGET

ESTIMATE OF EXPENDITURES FOR SCHOOL YEAR
BEGINNING JULY 1, 1939

Administration:

Salaries of district officers	$187.00
Superintendent's salary	320.00
Truant officer and school census	30.00
Expenses of administration	75.00

Instruction.

Teachers' salaries	5,750.00
Textbooks	200.00
Scholars' supplies	175.00
Flags and appurtenances	10.00
Other expenses of instruction	90.00

Operation and Maintenance:

Janitor service	247.00
Fuel	260.00
Light and janitor's supplies	160.00
Minor repairs and expenses	150.00

Auxiliary Agencies and Special Activities:

Health supervision (medical inspection)	$300.00
Transportation of pupils	2,242.00
High school tuition	2,400.00
Other special activities	25.00

Fixed Charges:

Per capita tax ($2 per pupil)	$310.00
Insurance and bonding	115.00

Construction and Equipment:

Alterations of old buildings	300.00
New equipment	150.00

Total	$13,496.00

Estimated Income (from sources other than taxation):

Dog tax	$195.09
Income from trust funds	133.92
Estimated balance June 30, 1939	400.00

Total	$729.01
Net amount to be raised by taxation	$12,766.99

This amount is higher than it should be by $25.00 as that sum has been deducted by selectmen from dog tax to pay dog officer.

Figures for comparison:

Amount raised for schools, 1938	$12,581.00
Average amount spent for last four years, (not counting Federal Aid for Quimby School)	12,088.74

ALICE D. SMITH,
ALISTON H. GRANT,
GRACE E. AINGER,
School Board of Sandwich.

TREASURER'S REPORT

Fiscal Year Ending June 30, 1938

Cash on hand June 30, 1937		$541.45
Received from Selectmen:		
Appropriations for current year	$12,370.00	
Dog tax	231.04	
Income from Trust Funds	133.92	
Received from State Treasurer:		
Federal Aid	1,154.94	
		$13,889.90
Total amount available for fiscal year		$14,431.35
Less School Board orders paid		13,403.78
Balance on hand as of June 30, 1938		$1,027.57

IDA L. ROGERS,
District Treasurer.

This is to certify that we have examined the books, vouchers, bank statements and other financial records of the treasurer of the school district of Sandwich and find them correct in all respects.

SUMNER B. CLARK,
July 12, 1938   *Auditor.*

REPORT OF THE SUPERINTENDENT OF SCHOOLS

To the Citizens of Sandwich:

This is my second annual report as your superintendent. It deals briefly with the following topics:

(a) Statistics of our schools.

(b) Buildings and grounds.

(c) Music instruction.

(d) Cost of high school tuition.

(e) Transportation of pupils.

STATISTICAL TABLE

STATISTICS FOR YEAR ENDING JUNE 30, 1938

Schools and Teachers	No. Half-days School in Session	Total Enrollment	No. Pupils (Average Membership)	Percent of Attendance	No. Tardinesses per Pupil	No. Pupils not Absent or Tardy
Center, Grammar (Glorie St. John Mason)	362	31	27.59	94.85	1.93	2
Center, Primary (Jeanne McKenzie Smith)	362	32	29.61	94.12	1.53	2
Chick's Corner (Rosealie Q. Burrows)	358	12	10.43	95.78	0.16	1
Lower Corner (Helen Weed)	358	21	18.57	94.07	0.71	2
North Sandwich (Agnes Mooney) (Leonard Smith)	360	22	19.00	96.00	0.18	0
Whiteface (Zellene Young)	360	10	9.37	96.28	1.60	2
Quimby School (H. F. Presby, Headmaster)	358	44	42.37	94.71	2.11	5
All Sandwich Schools (Total or average)	359.7	172	156.94	95.11	1.17	14
State of New Hampshire (Average)	353.4			94.7	0.9	

SCHOOL BUILDINGS AND GROUNDS

A decided improvement has been brought about at Whiteface by building a partition part way across the front of the room. This serves three purposes. It conceals the window in front of the pupils; it supports a new slate blackboard which has been needed there; and it provides a place for hanging wraps where they can be kept warm in cold weather.

The Lower Corner School has a half-acre of playground space, recently purchased. In spite of numerous stones and boulders, it provides a reasonably level space for baseball and other games.

Considering the enrollment of the school, the two-room school at Center Sandwich has the least satisfactory playground space. The drainage from an adjoining alder swamp covers the lower end with water at certain seasons, and the brownish color of this overflow has led some people to suspect sewage contamination. An examination by the State Laboratory of Hygiene proved that there was no indication of pollution; but the fact remains that the ground is swampy at the lower side where the swings are located, and that drainage ought to be provided. An article in the warrant provides opportunity for the voters to act on this matter at the district meeting.

MUSIC INSTRUCTION

This year, under the direction of Donald Musgrove, a music supervisor with several years of experience, our teachers are making a systematic effort to improve the work in music instruction. Mr. Musgrove spends one day each week in Sandwich, and devotes a period of time to each school, teaching a music class and assigning work to be carried on during the remainder of the week by the regular teacher. Results of this instruction are already evident. It is my belief that this work is very valuable and should be continued during the years to come.

HIGH SCHOOL TUITION COSTS

An unusually large eighth grade (18 pupils) will increase considerably the number who may be expected to attend high school next year. This accounts for the increased estimate of tuition cost indicated in the budget for 1939-1940.

TRANSPORTATION OF PUPILS

The law requires that a school district provide transportation for elementary pupils who live two miles or more from school. For younger children who live not quite two miles away, the trip to school on foot in severe weather presents a real hardship. School boards in past years have declined to make any provision for transportation in such cases, since it was not a legal requirement and no funds were provided for the purpose. It would seem to the writer that some provision for carrying these pupils, at least during the winter months, would be worthwhile. I believe the school board concurs in this opinion, and will present an article in the school warrant providing an opportunity for the district to vote on the matter.

ACKNOWLEDGMENTS

Citizens, teachers, school board, and pupils have shown the usual generous spirit of cooperation in various school activities, which is much appreciated.

The Parent-Teacher Association, Red Cross, and Sandwich Womans' Club assisted with the expense of hot lunches. The gift of a large United States flag to the Lower Corner School by Lieutenant Frank W. Walter, and a donation of $5.00 to each of the schools in town from Mr. and Mrs. Cleveland Weed, deserve our thanks. Let us continue in this fine spirit of mutual helpfulness.

Respectfully submitted,

ALMON W. BUSHNELL,
Superintendent.

GRADUATES, QUIMBY SCHOOL, 1938

Lawrence Quimby Beede	Amy Mae Shaw
Phoebe Rita Lewis	Pauline Vittum
Elizabeth Dorr Nixon	Walter Clark White

EIGHTH GRADE GRADUATES
CLASS OF 1938

Charles G. Burrows	Roland B. Jackson
James M. Burrows	Mary A. Lewis
Virginia Forristall	Thelma L. Robinson
Dennis W. Gilman	Kenneth D. Vittum
William G. Irvine	

ROLL OF PERFECT ATTENDANCE

Pupils present every day without tardiness for school year ending June 30, 1938:

Sylbert Ainger	Elizabeth Greene
Fred Bickford	Wilbur Greene
Lillian Bodge	Charles Knox
Virginia Bodge	Mary Knox
James Burrows	Earle Leach
Philip Elliott	Charles Peaslee
Richard Gray	Kenneth Vittum

ROLL OF PERFECT ATTENDANCE FOR HALF-YEAR

Pupils present every day without tardiness for first nineteen weeks of school year beginning September, 1938:

Fred Bickford, Jr.	Arthur Leach
Geraldine Bryant	Morton Martel
Jacqueline Bryant	Beulah Merrifield
Milton Bryant	Frank Moulton
Phyllis Bryant	Charlotte Nelson
Stewart Bryant	Kenneth Nelson
Charles Burrows	Wallace Nudd
Isabel Burrows	Carolyn Peaslee
Nelson Condon	Charles Peaslee
Jean Davis	David Peaslee
Earline Dearborne	Earle Peaslee
Jean Dearborne	Pearl Smith
Edward Elliott	Robert Smith
Philip Elliott	Howard Tilton
Elizabeth Gray	Lorraine Tilton
Richard Gray	Robert Balentine
Wilbur Greene	Cora Joe Vittum
William Irvine	June Vittum
Charles Knox	Janet Watson
Mary Knox	Richard Watson

REPORT OF SCHOOL NURSE

This report is a summary of the work done by the school nurse.

Pupils enrolled and inspected	119
Visits to schools	139
Visits to homes	152
Days spent in town	45¾
Transported to eye clinic	7
Transported to dental clinic	62
Transported to tonsil clinic	5

Dr. Thompson examined the first and fifth grades. The nurse inspected the other six grades. Dr. Quimby examined all pupils in the Quimby School.

Eye cases needing attention and taken care of by clinic rates were treated by Dr. R. A. Hernandez in Laconia. The Sandwich Chapter of the Red Cross made possible these corrections. Dr. Pottle very kindly permitted his dental hygienist to come to Sandwich and examine all children at the schools. At a later date she came to Sandwich and cleaned the teeth of all pupils who required only a cleaning to qualify for the state's honor roll. All other pupils were taken to Dr. Pottle's office for treatment. Thanks are due to all those who helped with the transportation problem by taking other people's children. A one hundred per cent dental correction was thus made possible.

Part of the tonsilectomies were done on pre-school children, thus getting them ready for the school age group.

Many thanks are due the Sandwich Red Cross Committee for their splendid co-operation. The cod liver oil provided by this organization has meant a very great deal in keeping the children fit. The prevalence of colds is much less and the children appear less fatigued at the close of the winter.

Sincere appreciation is extended to all who have helped complete this constructive and corrective health program.

Respectfully submitted,

EVA M. NELSON, R. N.,
School Nurse.

VITAL STATISTICS

To the Selectmen—In compliance with an act of Legislature passed June session, 1887, requiring clerks of towns and cities to furnish a transcript of the records of births, marriages, and deaths to the municipal officers for publication in the Annual Report, I hereby submit the following:

Births Registered in the Town of Sandwich for the year ending December 31, 1938.

Date	Name of the Child (if any)	Sex and Condition Male or Female	Living or Stillborn	No. of Children	Color	Name of Father	Maiden Name of Mother	Residence of Parents	Occupation of Father	Birthplace of Father	Birthplace of Mother
Jan. 25	Eugenia May	Female	Living	1	W	Langdon J. Ambrose	Ada M. Collins	Sandwich	Student	N. Sandwich, N.H.	Canaan, Vt.
Jan. 25	Richard Austin	Male	Living	1	W	Austin G. Burrows	Thelma M. Dumas	Sandwich	Salesman	C. Sandwich, N.H.	Woburn, Mass.
Feb. 10	Ruth Lena	Female	Living	2	W	Fred E. Barnes	Florence M. Whiting	Sandwich	Laborer	Tamworth, N. H.	S.Tamworth,N.H.
Feb. 10	Eleanor May*	Female	Living	3	W	Fred E. Barnes	Florence M. Whiting	Sandwich	Laborer	Tamworth, N. H.	S.Tamworth,N.H.
Feb. 16	Janet Carrol	Female	Living	5	W	Ernest E. MacDonald	Ethel B. Diack	Sandwich	Laborer	Union, N. H.	Quincy, Mass.
Mar. 26	Donald	Male	Living	4	W	Elziar J. Martelle	Beatrice M. Palmer	Sandwich	Farmer	St. Monique, Can.	Sandwich, N. H.
Mar. 28	Ronald Wilfred	Male	Living	3	W	Wilfred J. Sturgeon	Erma Stokes	Sandwich	Laborer	Van Buren, Me.	Harrison, Me.
April 27	Lorraine Anne	Female	Living	12	W	Clarence R. Plummer	Luella M. Sturgis	Sandwich	Laborer	Sandwich, N. H.	Sandwich, N. H.
May 27	Genevieve Ellen	Female	Living	5	W	Clifford R. Matthews	Marjorie T. Bartley	Sandwich	Woodworker	Craftsbury, Vt.	S. Reading, Vt.
June 29	Bette Ann	Female	Living	5	W	Forrest E. Davis	Charlotte Hoag	Sandwich	Carpenter	Wakefield, N. H.	Sandwich, N.H.
July 3	Patricia Florence	Female	Living	1	W	Francis C. Mudgett	Ruth A. Shaw	Sandwich	Laborer	Sandwich, N. H.	Moult'nboro, N.H
Sept. 3	Doris	Female	Living	3	W	Paul A. Taylor	Marion Gray	Sandwich	Laborer	Sandwich, N. H.	Sanbornton, N.H.
Sept. 19	Bruce Elliott	Male	Living	4	W	Fred C. Mudgett	Marion Elliott	Sandwich	Truckman	Sandwich, N. H.	Sandwich, N. H.
Sept. 29	Donna Averena	Female	Living	1	W	Merton H. Plume	Eleanor A. Slack	Sandwich	Pile Driver	Groton, N. H.	Corinth, Vt.
Oct. 29	Melvin Orace	Male	Living	1	W	Orace R. Littlefield	Beatrice M. Johnson	Sandwich	Laborer	Brownfield, Me.	Tamworth, N. H.
Dec. 14	Rita Anne	Female	Living	1	W	Wilbur E. Martin	Dora E. Peaslee	Sandwich	Laborer	Sandwich, N. H.	Sandwich, N. H.

Date	Pce of Me	N me and Surname of Gm and Bride and Pe of Bth at Time of Marriage	Age in Years	Color	Gn and Bde	Pce of Bth	N me of Parents	Pce of Bits	N a, i cBd en by P
June 18	Sandwich, N. H.	Bd Leo Dumas Sdch, N. H. Bth all Read Sdch, N. H.	24 25	W W	Slt At Home	Salem, Ms. Bth, Ms.	Gy Dumas Ins Bfe Inn H. Bd Mk	Be Rivers, G. Greenville, N. H. W. Somerville, Ms.	A. Ge Blt ign C. Sandwich, N. H.
July 10	Sdh, N. H.	Wr Leroy We Sdch, N. H. Fle Ella Beede Lynn, M.	54 55	W W	Fr Mt	Hn, Ms. Lyn, Ms.	Aske R. Me Wl er Me Ca Powers My A. Ry	Phillipston, Ms. Hin, Ms. Lynn, Ms. Jn, M.	A. Ge Blt Sn C.
Aug. 6	Sdch, N. H.	Robert Ge Dustin Sdch, N. H.	24	W	Jy	Boscawen, N. H.	Rnk B Dustin My A. Bit	Hebron, N. H. Sdl, N. H.	H. D. G. Clergyman, Curch,
Aug. 27	Sandwich, N. H.	Ely i Wn Heard Sdch, N. H. Be Os Read Sdch, N. H.	21 24	W W	Wd Wl er At Home	Bth, Ms. St Anthony's Newfoundl nd	Bin A. dHrd Hin P. ad fin Leon H. ad baie R. allok	Wr. Ms. W. Somerville, Ms. W, R. I.	A. Ge n Sdl, N. H.
O t 10	Boscawen, N. H.	nhrd oln nSth Sdl, N. H. Es Agnes Dwyer Gd, N. H.	27 23	W W	Tr Tr	Gd, N. H. New York, N. Y.	John N. Smith Lulu M. Shld Me J. Dwyer Hn Oln	Newport, N. H. Gln, N. H. Gd, N. H. Norway	t A. Hayes, Sm Boscawen, N. H.
Nov. 2	Mo, N. H.	Wr Es ky Sdch, N. H. Emma Sophia Karlin New Britain, one	51 43	W W	Gr Gk	Sdl, N. H. B, v wn	Es J. Kin Bth L. Gk Gf M. Karlin Aa R. Gin	Sandwich, N. H. Sandwich, N. H. Bratton, v Sn Bratton, Sn	K H Underwood, Mt. Episcopal Mr, Mo. N. H.
Nov. 12	sdh, N. H.	Hazen one Sdch, N. H. Ellen Elizabeth Bhr Sdch, N. H.	18 18	W W	Laborer t Home	Ge, N. H. v dth, N. H.	Willie R. Be Ga B. Ms Ge Cle R. Bhr Luella Me Sns	Be, N. H. A, N. H. Hin, N. H. Sdl, N. H.	Rev. F. G. Paddon, Gd d Mr, dth, N. H.

Deaths Registered in the Town of Sandwich for the year ending December 31, 1938.

Date of Death	Name of Deceased	Age (Years)	Age (Months)	Age (Days)	Place of Birth	Color	Single, Married or widowed	Male or Female	Occupation	Place of Birth (Father)	Place of Birth (Mother)	Name of Father	Maiden Name of Mother
Feb. 25	Jennie A. Vittum	87	5	17	Salem, N. H.	W	W	Female	Housewife	Sandwich, N. H.	Sandwich, N. H.	Aaron Wilson	Allie Bailey
Mar. 11	Charles B. Hoyt	78	3	9	Sandwich, N. H.	W	W	Male	Farmer	St.	Me. Can	Burleigh Hoyt	Caroline Quimby
Mar. 27	Donald Martelle	64	.. 3	29	Sandwich, N. H.	W	S	Male	....	.... Me	Smith, N. H.	Elzear Martelle	Beatrice Palmer
Apr. 11	Amey M. Munn	81	7	17	Smith, N. H.	W	M	Female	At Home	Sandwich, N. H.	Smith, N. H.	Hazel Vittum	Ghia Wallace
Apr. 18	Alice N. Blanchard	73	10	28	Sandwich, N. H.	W	W	Female	Farmer	Batch,	Smith, N. H.	Arthur Quby	Winnie Bryer
May 9	Herbert Palmer	84	2	14	Sandwich, N. H.	W	W	Male	Farmer	Sandwich, N. H.	Moultonboro, N. H.	Ambrose Palmer	Carolyn Milton
May 20	White H. Penniman	79		16	Me. Me.	W	W	Male		Lebanon, M	Sandwich, N. H.	Robert Penniman	Carolyn Wallace
May 31	Olive E. Miller	84	1	21	Tuftonboro, N. H.	W	W	Female	Housewife	Ireland	U. S. A.	David M. Brock	Emmeline Ricker
June 5	Annie M. Plummer	86	7	24	Sandwich, N. H.	W	W	Female	House pr	Sandwich, N. H.	Sandwich, N. H.	Daniel Leary	Mary Swett
June 6	Clara Ann Bean	77	7	8	Sandwich, N. H.	W	W	Female	Housewife	Sandwich, N. H.	Sandwich, N. H.	Stephen Varn	Ruth Tappan
June 11	Carrie I. Gitting	70	6	3	Boston, Mass.	W	M	Idle	House'pr	Baden-Baden, Gr.	Baden-Baden, Gr.	Lemuel F. Vittum	Philipina Wk
June 22	Frank Neff	79	11	11	Madison, N. H.	W	M	Idle	Gardner	Madison, N. H.	Fryeburg, Me.	Frank A. Neff	Ghia Wallace
July 10	Ada H. Sullivan	82	9	21	Ojibay, Sweden	W	W	Female	House'pr	Sweden	Sweden	John A. Forrest	Eliza Richardson
July 18	Andrew J. Carlson	78	5	2	Batch, N. H.	W	M	Male	Store	Sandwich, N. H.	Sanford, Me.		
July 18	Julia A. Moulton	57	8	19	Sandwich, N. H.	W	W	Female	Housewife			David Tilton	Susan W. Hill
Aug. 15	Maude L. Elliott	91	4	4	Sandwich, N. H.	W	M	Female	Housewife	Sandwich, N. H.	Wolfeboro, N. H.	Charles Mitchell	Susan Fullerton
Sept. 2	Stanley F. Quby	80	2	16	Boston, Mass.	W	M	Male	Farmer	Sandwich, N. H.	Tamworth, N. H.	William Quby	Mary Watson
Oct. 18	Mary E. Gotshall	65	11	26	Lakeport, N. H.	W	W	Female	Housewife	Waterboro, Me.	Boston, Mass.	William T. Watt	Frances Hoyt
Oct. 29	Frank W. Davis	78	6	20	Boston, N. H.	W	M	Idle	Ther	Lakeport, N. H.	Mb, N. H.	Samuel Davis	Mary Pickering
Nov. 19	Frank L. Crowell	75	3	18	Mon, N. H.	W	W	Idle	Laborer	Hyde Park, Vt.	Sandwich, N. H.	Harum Crowell	Marilla Brown

I hereby certify that the above and foregoing is a true transcript of all the births, marriages, and deaths that have been reported to me for the year ending December 31, 1938.

PERLEY C. KNOX, Town Clerk.